Christ United Methodist Church

Erie, Pennsylvania

814-833-6398

Extends a Cordial Welcome to All Services

SUNDAY

Traditional Worship ....8:15 a.m.

Sunday School All Ages ....9:30 a.m.

Blended Worship...10:45 a.m.

OFFICE HOURS

Monday-Friday – 9:00 a.m.-2:00 p.m.

Michelle L. Wobrak, Pastor

A

Expression of Appreciation

Our organization, the compilers and sponsors of this cookbook, would like to thank and express our sincere appreciation to the many people in the community who gave so generously of their time and energy in collecting and submitting recipes and assisting with the sale of our cookbooks. Without their help, this book would not have been possible.

**The Ghana Team
"2009"**

DEDICATION

We dedicate this book to all cooks. In our homes today, as always, life is centered around the kitchen. It is with this thought in mind that we, the sponsors, have compiled these recipes. Some of the recipes are treasured family keepsakes and some are new; however, they all reflect the love of good cooking.

Our thanks to all those who generously contributed their favorite recipes. Without their help, this book would never have been possible.

We hope you will enjoy the many outstanding and treasured recipes on the pages that follow.

Ghana Mission Team
"2009"

TABLE OF CONTENTS

 In Loving Memory

155308

Appetizers, Relishes
and Pickles

Recipe Favorites

Recipe Title:_____ _____

_____ _____

_____ _____

_____ _____

_____ _____

_____ _____

_____ _____

_____ _____

_____ _____

_____ _____

Family Favorites

Page No.

Recipe Title:_____ _____

_____ _____

_____ _____

_____ _____

_____ _____

Notes:_____

_____

_____

_____

APPETIZERS, RELISHES & PICKLES

🌿 TANGY CHEESE BALLS 🌿

4 oz. Blue cheese
1 (8 oz.) plastic container
  medium soft sharp
  Cheddar
1 (8 oz.) pkg. cream cheese

1 Tbsp. grated onion
½ tsp. Worcestershire sauce
½ c. pecans, chopped
⅛ c. chopped parsley or
  dried flakes

Keep cheese at room temperature. Mix cheese well (by hand or mixer) with onion and Worcestershire sauce. Add parsley and ½ of the pecans. Chill in refrigerator 1 or 2 hours. Form into about 4 balls and roll in rest of the pecans. Can also be wrapped in foil and frozen.

Agnes Billisits

🌿 CEREAL MIX 🌿

1 pkg. pretzel sticks
1 pkg. Rice Chex
1 pkg. Cheerios
1 pkg. Wheat Chex
1 lb. butter or oleo

1 lb. nuts
1 tsp. garlic salt
1 tsp. Worcestershire sauce
1 tsp. celery salt
1 tsp. onion salt

Melt butter; add salts and pour over cereal. Heat in covered roaster at 225° for 1 ½ hours, tossing occasionally.

Agnes Billisits

🌿 BUFFALO CHICKEN DIP 🌿

1 (8 oz.) pkg. cream cheese
1 pkg. Cheddar cheese (2 c.)
1 c. Ranch dressing

1 can chicken
hot sauce to taste or buffalo
  wing sauce

Serve with tortilla chips or crackers.

Kathy Lore

❧ PEPPERONI DIP ❧

2 cans cream of celery soup
2 (8 oz.) pkg. cream cheese
  (soft)

pepperoni (desired amount),
  chopped up

Put ingredients in crock-pot and stir occasionally. Serve with tortilla chips or crackers.

❧ CARAMEL APPLE PIZZA ❧
(Prep: 40 Minutes + Cooling; Yield: 12 Slices.)

¼ c. butter, softened
¼ c. sugar
¼ c. packed brown sugar
1 egg
2 Tbsp. canola oil
1 Tbsp. light corn syrup

1 tsp. vanilla extract
1 c. whole-wheat pastry flour
¾ c. all-purpose flour
½ tsp. baking powder
¼ tsp. salt
¼ tsp. ground cinnamon

Topping:

1 (8 oz.) pkg. fat-free cream
  cheese
¼ c. packed brown sugar
½ tsp. ground cinnamon
½ tsp. vanilla extract

3 medium Granny Smith
  apples, thinly sliced
¼ c. fat-free caramel ice
  cream topping
¼ c. chopped unsalted dry
  roasted peanuts

In a large mixing bowl, cream butter and sugars. Beat in the egg, oil, corn syrup and vanilla. Combine the flours, baking powder, salt and cinnamon; gradually add to creamed mixture and mix well. Press dough onto a 14-inch pizza pan coated with cooking spray. Bake at 350° for 12 to 15 minutes or until lightly browned. Cool on a wire rack.

In a small mixing bowl, beat the cream cheese, brown sugar, cinnamon and vanilla until smooth. Spread over crust. Arrange apples over the top. Drizzle with caramel topping; sprinkle with peanuts. Serve immediately.

Louise Johnson

❧ FRESH FRUIT DIP ❧

1 (8 oz.) pkg. cream cheese
1 (7 oz.) jar Marshmallow
  Crème

1 Tbsp. orange juice or
  orange juice concentrate

Beat all ingredients together until smooth. Serve with your favorite fresh fruits.

Helen McKenzie

❧ FRUIT ON A STICK ❧

1 (8 oz.) pkg. cream cheese,
  softened
1 (7 oz.) jar Marshmallow
  Creme

3 to 4 Tbsp. milk
halved strawberries
melon and kiwifruit, cut into
  bite-size pieces

Mix cream cheese, Marshmallow Creme and milk until smooth. Thread fruit on wooden skewers. Serve with dip. Yield: 1 ½ cups dip.

Leigh Ann Gigliotti

❧ CLAM DIP ❧

1 ½ c. minced clams
  (canned)
4 oz. cream cheese

1 tsp. Worcestershire sauce
1 Tbsp. grated onion
1 egg white, beaten stiff

Whip cream cheese until smooth. Add other ingredients except egg white. Mix well. Then fold in beaten egg white. Pile on Ritz crackers. Bake 3 minutes at 450°. Serve immediately.

Jackie Wallace

❧ CORN DIP ❧

1 c. mayo
1 c. sour cream

2 c. fancy cheese
1 can Mexican corn

Could add green onions and Tabasco sauce. Serve with chips/crackers.

Patti Sitter

❧ APPLE DIP ❧

1 (8 oz.) pkg. cream cheese,
  softened
¾ c. brown sugar

¼ c. granulated sugar
1 Tbsp. vanilla

Blend and enjoy with a firm, tart apple like Granny Smith.

Cindy Andrus

❧ HOT TACO DIP ❧

1 (8 oz.) cream cheese,
  softened
1 lb. ground beef
1 pkg. taco seasoning

1 jar salsa
1 c. or more shredded
  Cheddar cheese

Spread cream cheese in 9 x 13 pan. Brown ground beef with taco seasoning (following directions on package). Spread ground beef mixture over cream cheese; top with salsa and Cheddar cheese. Bake at 350° until heated and cheese melts, 15 to 20 minutes. Serve with corn chips.

Linda Holman

❧ RANCH HAM ROLL-UPS ❧

2 (8 oz.) pkg. cream cheese,
  softened
1 envelope Ranch salad
  dressing mix

3 green onions, chopped
11 flour tortillas (8-inches)
22 thin slices deli ham

In a small mixing bowl, beat the cream cheese and salad dressing mix until smooth. Add onions; mix well. Spread about 3 tablespoons over each tortilla; top each with 2 ham slices. Roll up tightly and wrap in plastic wrap. Refrigerate until firm. Unwrap and cut into ¾-inch slices. Yield: about 7 ½ dozen.

Louise Johnson

❧ CHEESE PENNIES ❧

2 c. shredded sharp Cheddar
  cheese
2 c. flour
1 c. melted butter

1 tsp. salt
½ tsp. red pepper
2 c. Rice Krispies

Combine Cheddar cheese, flour, melted butter, salt and red pepper in large bowl; mix well. Stir in Rice Krispies. Shape into penny-sized circles on lightly greased baking sheet. Bake at 375° for 10 minutes or until slightly brown around edges. Yields approximately 60.

Audrey Evans

☘ COCKTAIL PUFFS ☘

1 c. water
½ c. margarine
1 c. flour

¼ tsp. salt
4 eggs

Bring water and margarine to a rolling boil. Stir in flour and beat vigorously over low heat (approximately 1 minute) until it forms a ball. Remove from heat and beat in eggs one at a time until smooth and glossy. Drop by teaspoon onto ungreased baking sheet. Bake at 400° for 8 minutes and then reduce heat to 350° and continue baking 10 to 12 minutes or until puffed and golden brown and dry. Cool on a wire rack slowly and away from a draft. When cool and just before serving, fill with ham, chicken, tuna or egg salad.

Audrey Evans

☘ ZUCCHINI APPETIZERS ☘

3 c. thinly sliced unpared
   zucchini (about 4 small)
1 c. Bisquick baking mix
½ c. finely chopped onion
½ c. grated Parmesan cheese
½ tsp. salt
½ tsp. dried marjoram or
   oregano

dash of pepper
½ c. vegetable oil
2 Tbsp. snipped parsley
½ tsp. seasoned salt
1 clove garlic, chopped
4 eggs, slightly beaten

Heat oven to 350°. Grease 13 x 9 x 2-inch oblong pan. Mix all ingredients; spread in pan. Bake until golden brown (about 25 minutes). Cut into pieces, about 2 x 1-inch squares. Yields 4 dozen pieces.

Audrey Evans

SUGAR-COATED PEANUTS

1 c. sugar
½ c. water

2 c. shelled raw peanuts

Combine sugar and water in saucepan. Cook over medium heat until sugar is dissolved, stirring constantly. Add peanuts. Cook until peanuts are completely coated and no syrup remains. Stir frequently. Spread on ungreased baking sheet. Separate peanuts with fork. Bake at 300° for 30 minutes. Stir every 10 minutes. Yield: 16 servings.

Audrey Evans

HIDDEN VALLEY ROAD OYSTER CRACKERS

16 oz. plain oyster crackers
1 pkg. Hidden Valley
  Ranch/buttermilk recipe
  salad dressing mix

¼ tsp. lemon pepper
1 tsp. dill weed
¼ tsp. garlic powder
1 c. salad oil

Combine Ranch mix and oil. Add dill weed, garlic powder and lemon pepper. Pour over crackers. Stir to coat. Place in 250° oven for 15 to 20 minutes.

TEXAS CAVIAR

2 cans black beans, rinsed
1 can pinto beans, rinsed
1 can white corn, drained
1 can diced green chilies

1 each: red, green and
  orange peppers
1 small red onion, diced
1 small bunch cilantro,
  chopped

Dressing:

½ c. rice or white vinegar
½ c. olive oil

½ tsp. garlic powder
sugar to taste (⅓ c. or so)

Bring to a boil; let cool and pour over above mixture. Serve with tortilla chips or crackers or as a relish.

Gail Sollman

TACO DIP

1 pkg. taco seasoning
1 (8 oz.) cream cheese,
  softened

½ c. sour cream

APPETIZERS, RELISHES & PICKLES

Mix well and spread on serving plate. Top with shredded lettuce and shredded Cheddar cheese. Add diced red and green pepper, tomatoes and onion, also sliced green and black olives. Serve with white corn chips.

Nancy Root

❧ REUBEN DIP ❧

1 lb. chip chop ham, cut into
  bite-sized pieces
1 (8 oz.) pkg. cream cheese
1 c. shredded Swiss cheese,
  divided

1 whole chopped onion
  (large)
10 to 15 oz. can sauerkraut,
  drained

Mix all, reserving ½ cup Swiss cheese. Bake at 375° for 40 minutes, covered with foil, 20 minutes without foil, adding remaining cheese to top for last 20 minutes.

(I mix with a mixer as it breaks sauerkraut into smaller pieces.)

Cindy Andrus

❧ HOT CORN DIP WITH CRISPY ❧ TORTILLA CHIPS

2 Tbsp. unsalted butter
3 ½ c. corn kernels (fresh or
  canned), well drained
½ tsp. salt
⅛ tsp. freshly ground black
  pepper
1 c. finely chopped yellow
  onion
½ c. finely chopped red bell
  pepper
¼ c. chopped green onions
  (green and white parts)

1 jalapeno, seeded and
  minced
2 tsp. minced garlic
½ to 1 c. mayonnaise
4 oz. Monterey Jack or
  Cheddar, shredded
4 oz. sharp Cheddar,
  shredded
¼ tsp. cayenne
tortilla chips (for dipping)

Melt 1 tablespoon of the butter in a large heavy skillet over medium-high heat. Add the corn, salt and pepper. Cook, stirring occasionally, until the kernels turn deep golden brown, about 5 minutes. Transfer to a bowl. Melt the remaining tablespoon of butter in the skillet. Add the onion and bell pepper and cook, stirring often, until the onions are wilted, about 2 minutes. Add the green onions, jalapeno and garlic and cook, stirring, for 2 minutes or until the vegetables are softened. Transfer to the bowl with the corn. Add the mayonnaise, ½ of the Monterey Jack and half of the Cheddar and the cayenne and mix well. Pour into an 8-inch square baking dish and sprinkle the remaining cheese on top. Bake at 350° until bubbly and golden brown, 10 to 12 minutes. Serve hot with the chips.

Linda Holman

❦ SWEET AND SOUR CHICKEN ❦ WINGS

60 chicken wings
12 oz. bottle chili sauce or ketchup
10 oz. jar grape jelly
2 Tbsp. lemon juice
½ tsp. garlic powder

16 oz. can sweet and sour sauce
7 ½ oz. jar junior baby food peaches
¼ tsp. powdered ginger

Preheat oven to 350°. Line a shallow roasting pan with heavy foil. Place wings in roasting pan. In a medium saucepan, bring remaining ingredients to a boil, stirring occasionally, until jelly melts. Pour ¾ of sauce over wings. Bake at 350° for 1 ½ or 2 hours or until brown and crispy, basting and turning often.

May be refrigerated, covered, for 2 days. Refrigerate extra sauce separately.

May be frozen. Sauce may be frozen. Bring to room temperature. Brush wings with reserved sauce. Bake at 350° for 20 to 30 minutes or until heated through.

Michelle Wobrak

❦ SPINACH DIP ❦

1 envelope vegetable soup mix
1 (8 oz.) container sour cream
1 c. mayonnaise

1 (10 oz.) pkg. frozen spinach, thawed and squeezed dry
1 (8 oz.) can water chestnuts, drained and chopped (optional)

Combine and mix all ingredients. Chill 2 hours. Serve with pumpernickel bread, vegetables, crackers, etc. Makes 3 cups.

Kathy Lore

❧ SPINACH ARTICHOKE DIP ❧

½ c. sour cream
½ c. mayonnaise
½ c. grated Parmesan cheese
½ c. Mozzarella cheese
1 to 2 tsp. minced garlic

1 (10 oz.) pkg. frozen chopped spinach, thawed and squeezed dry
1 (14 oz.) can artichoke hearts

Combine all ingredients. Place in shallow casserole dish. Bake at 325° for 15 to 20 minutes (may be microwaved for a few minutes). Serve with tortilla chips or veggie tray.

Gail Sollman

❧ PUMPKIN DIP ❧

2 pkg. (8 oz.) cream cheese, softened
1 c. powdered sugar

1 small can pumpkin
½ to 1 tsp. ginger
1 tsp. cinnamon

Mix cream cheese and sugar with mixer. Add pumpkin and spices; blend well. Use gingersnaps to dip.

Kathy Lore

❧ CHILI CHEESE DIP ❧

1 can chili (with or without beans)
1 (8 oz.) pkg. cream cheese (soft)

2 c. shredded Cheddar cheese
tortilla chips

Spread cream cheese in a Pyrex pie plate. Spread chili over cheese. Sprinkle Cheddar cheese on top. Microwave until Cheddar cheese is melted. Serve with tortilla chips.

❧ EASY MEXICAN PIZZAS ❧

1 pkg. large tortillas (flour)
2 c. Mexican blend shredded cheese
1 Tbsp. vegetable oil
1 lb. skinless chicken breasts or hamburger, cut chicken into small pieces

1 pkg. taco seasoning mix
1 (1 lb.) can refried beans
taco sauce
toppings (chopped tomatoes, sliced green onions, black olives, sliced)

Preheat oven to 375°. Place 5 tortillas on greased baking sheets. Sprinkle each with ¼ cup cheese. Place remaining tortillas on top of cheese. Heat vegetable oil in large skillet over medium heat. Add chicken; cook 4 to 5 minutes, until done. Add 2 tablespoons seasoning mix and 1 tablespoon water; mix well. Remove from heat. Combine refried beans, remaining taco mix and 1 tablespoon of water in a small bowl. Spread about ¼ cup bean mixture on each tortilla. Layer with a drizzle of taco sauce, chicken mixture, remaining cheese and desired toppings. Bake for 5 to 8 minutes or until cheese is melted. Makes 5 pizzas.

Kathy Lore

CHICKEN WING DIP

8 oz. cream cheese
1 Tbsp. butter
¼ to ⅓ c. Red Hot sauce
1 c. shredded chicken

dash of salt, pepper, garlic
powder and celery salt
1 c. shredded Cheddar

Place in greased casserole. Bake 20 minutes at 350°.

Lynn Delio

CORN CURL SNACK

2 pkg. Troyer Farms puff
curls
2 sticks butter

2 c. brown sugar
½ c. Karo syrup

Place puff curls in roaster. In a saucepan, melt butter, brown sugar and syrup. Boil for 5 minutes; remove mixture from heat. Stir in ½ teaspoon baking soda. Pour mixture over curls. Bake, uncovered, for 1 hour at 250°, stirring several times while baking.

Lynn Delio

MEAT CHEESE LOAF

1 lb. ground beef
¾ c. diced American cheese
⅓ c. chopped onion
¼ c. chopped green pepper
1 tsp. salt
1 egg

¼ tsp. pepper
½ tsp. celery salt
¼ tsp. paprika
1 ¼ c. evaporated milk
½ c. bread crumbs

Place meat, cheese, onion, green pepper, seasonings, milk and bread crumbs in bowl. Beat egg and add. Stir ingredients until mixed; mixture will be soft. Spoon into greased loaf pan. Bake at 350° about 1 ½ hours. Leave in pan until bubbling stops, then remove to platter.

Lynn Delio

❦ CHEESE BALL ❦

1 jar Roka Blue cheese
1 jar Old English

8 oz. Philly cheese
½ tsp. garlic salt

Soften up. Mix with hands (it's easier). Roll in chopped nuts and parsley (optional).

Lynn Delio

❦ TACO DIP ❦

1 lb. hamburger
1 pkg. taco seasoning
1 c. hot taco sauce
2 (8 oz.) pkg. cream cheese
   (soft)

1 large French onion dip
1 head lettuce
2 tomatoes
1 pkg. taco cheese (2 c.)

Fry hamburger and drain. Add taco sauce and seasoning. Cool. Mix cream cheese and onion dip and spread on bottom of 9 x 13 dish. Cover with hamburger and cheese. Cut lettuce and tomatoes into small pieces. Put lettuce and tomatoes over cheese. Serve with tortilla chips.

❦ PINWHEELS ❦

2 (8 oz.) pkg. cream cheese
1 large pkg. Ranch dressing
   mix
2 green onions, minced
4 (12-inch) flour tortillas

1 (4 oz.) jar pimentos,
   drained
1 (4 oz.) can green chiles,
   diced
1 (2 oz.) can black olives,
   sliced

Cream together cream cheese, dressing mix and green onions. Drain pimentos, chilies and olives and blot dry on paper towels. Spread cheese mixture on tortillas; sprinkle vegetables on. Roll tightly. Chill 2 hours. Cut into 1-inch pieces.

❧ PICKLED EGGS ❧

2 c. beet juice (3 cans beets)
2 c. sugar
2 c. cider vinegar
3 tsp. salt

½ tsp. pepper
2 bay leaves
20 cloves

Boil juice for 5 minutes. Add 3 dozen eggs and beets.

❧ STAINED GLASS WINDOW ❧
S'MORES

1 stick margarine (¼ lb.)
12 oz. chocolate chips
(Nestle's)
10 ½ oz. pkg. miniature
colored marshmallows

1 c. finely chopped nuts
coconut (can be colored with
food coloring)

Melt margarine and chocolate chips in microwave and
let cool slightly. Then add to the marshmallows and nuts
and mix well. Sprinkle coconut on waxed paper; shape into
2 or 3 rolls and cover with coconut. Refrigerate.

Agnes Billisits

❧ SMORES BARS ❧

3 c. graham cracker crumbs
¾ c. margarine
1 c. sugar

3 c. mini marshmallows
2 c. chocolate chips

Combine butter, 2 cups crumbs and sugar. Press into a
greased 9 x 13 pan. Sprinkle with chocolate chips and
marshmallows. Top with remaining 1 cup crumbs. Press
firmly. Bake at 375° for 10 minutes. Remove from oven and
press firmly with spatula. Cool and cut.

Soups, Salads and Sauces

Recipe Favorites

Recipe Title:_____ _____

_____ _____

_____ _____

_____ _____

_____ _____

_____ _____

_____ _____

_____ _____

_____ _____

Family Favorites

Page No.

Recipe Title:_____ _____

_____ _____

_____ _____

_____ _____

_____ _____

Notes:_____

_____

_____

_____

SOUPS, SALADS & SAUCES

💐 TACO SOUP 💐

1 lb. ground beef
1 medium onion
1 pkg. taco seasoning
1 pkg. Hidden Valley Ranch
    dressing (dry)
1 (15 oz.) can pinto beans

1 (15 oz.) can spicy chili
    beans
1 can corn
2 (15 oz.) cans stewed
    tomatoes (Mexican style)

Brown ground beef with onion. Add remaining ingredients. Don't drain any of the beans or corn. Simmer for 1 hour and serve with baked corn chips.

Weight Watchers - 2 points per cup.

Tammie Wadding

💐 FAT BURNING SOUP 💐

1 ½ c. sliced carrots
1 c. chopped onion
6 c. fat-free chicken/beef/
    veggie broth
1 tsp. each basil and oregano
2 cans peeled/diced tomatoes
    (including juice)

1 c. chopped celery
1 stick butter
1 small head cabbage, diced
2 cans French sliced
    seasoned green beans
1 tsp. pepper blend

Saute carrots, onion and celery in butter on low until tender and onions are clear. In deep pan, add all ingredients; bring to a boil for 10 minutes. Reduce heat and simmer, covered, for 45 minutes to an hour. Veggies should be tender but not mushy. Makes 18 to 20 servings. Can be frozen. Keeps in refrigerator for a week to 10 days.

Karen Souder

POTATO CHEESE SOUP

2 c. cubed potatoes
½ c. chopped celery
½ c. hot water
¼ tsp. salt
1 ½ c. milk
1 Tbsp. fresh parsley

1 c. chopped carrots
½ c. chopped onion
1 chicken bouillon cube
⅛ tsp. pepper
1 c. shredded sharp cheese
    or more

Combine potatoes, carrots, celery, onion, water, bouillon cube, salt and pepper. Heat until vegetables are tender. Pour into a blender and mix until coarsely pureed. Return to pot and add milk and cheese. Heat until cheese melts. This is a to taste soup so more cheese is to your taste.

Betty Ann Smith

VEGETABLE CHICKEN CHOWDER

1 c. broccoli flowerets (can
    also use frozen chopped
    broccoli)
1 c. frozen whole kernel corn
½ c. water
¼ c. chopped onion
2 c. milk

1 ½ c. chopped cooked
    chicken or turkey
1 can condensed cream of
    potato soup
¾ c. shredded Cheddar
    cheese (extra for
    garnishing)
dash of pepper

In a large saucepan, combine broccoli, corn, water and onion. Bring to boiling. Reduce heat and simmer, covered, for 8 to 10 minutes (until vegetables are tender). Do not drain. Stir milk, chicken (turkey), potato soup, cheese and pepper into vegetable mixture. Cook and stir over medium heat until cheese melts and mixture is heated through. Sprinkle each serving with the extra cheese.

Helen McKenzie

CHEESE BROCCOLI SOUP

2 large potatoes, diced
1 ½ c. chopped onion
1 bunch fresh broccoli,
    chopped or 1 bag frozen
1 c. diced carrots
4 c. water

½ stick margarine
chicken bouillon cubes or
    chicken soup base (amount
    needed for 4 c. stock)
1 c. chopped celery

Mix above and cook until tender. Heat 2 cups milk and ½ cup flour in small saucepan until smooth. Stir gradually into vegetables and broth. Add 3 cups Cheddar, shredded. Cook and stir until cheese melts. Also good with some cauliflower added.

Cindy Andrus

❧ HAMBURG BARLEY VEGETABLE ❧ SOUP

1 ½ lb. hamburg	½ c. chopped green peppers
6 c. water	½ c. barley
3 tsp. beef bouillon	2 bay leaves
2 c. sliced carrots	¼ c. ketchup
1 ½ c. chopped onions	3 c. tomatoes (canned)
1 ½ c. chopped celery	8 oz. can tomato sauce

Brown hamburg; drain well. Stir in remaining ingredients and cook about 1 hour.

Carol Wingerter

❧ CLAM CHOWDER ❧

6 strips bacon, diced and browned in kettle	2 medium size potatoes, diced
1 medium onion	2 c. half and half and 1 of milk
some celery (including leaves)	seasonings (parsley flakes, pepper, celery salt)
1 small jar clam sauce plus liquid from 2 cans clams	½ stick margarine

Dice bacon and brown in kettle. Chop onion and some celery and saute in bacon grease. Add clam juice plus liquid from 2 cans clams and potatoes and cook this about 10 to 15 minutes. Add half and half, milk and seasonings. Add margarine. Add clams and heat. Cook about 1 ½ hours in all.

Agnes Billisits

❧ WHITE BEAN AND HAM SOUP ❧

2 (15 ½ oz.) cans Great Northern beans, rinsed and drained	2 Tbsp. butter or margarine
2 medium carrots, diced	2 ¼ c. water
1 small onion, chopped	1 ½ c. diced ham
	1 bay leaf

Mash one can of beans and set aside. Saute carrots and onion in butter until tender. Stir in all remaining ingredients. Cook until heated through.

Cindy Andrus

EASY VEGETABLE SOUP

1 lb. ground meat
1 can V-8 juice
1 can of water

1 pkg. mixed frozen
  vegetables
2 pkg. dry noodle soup mix

Cook and drain ground meat. Add juice, water, vegetables and dry noodle soup mix and heat.

Wilma Kenny

WISCONSIN SAUSAGE SOUP

½ c. butter
1 onion, chopped
1 carrot, chopped
1 tsp. minced garlic
1 c. all-purpose flour
2 c. chicken broth
2 c. milk
¾ c. beer
1 tsp. Worcestershire sauce

½ tsp. salt
½ tsp. dry mustard
1 bay leaf
7 oz. Cheddar cheese,
  shredded
3 oz. Swiss cheese, shredded
½ lb. Hillshire Farm smoked
  sausage

Melt butter in medium saucepan over medium heat. Add onion, carrot and garlic; sauté until softened. Add flour; cook 5 minutes, stirring often. Add chicken broth, milk, beer, Worcestershire sauce, salt, mustard and bay leaf. Reduce heat to low; cook until soup has thickened, whisking often. Slowly whisk cheeses into soup until combined and smooth. Cut sausage lengthwise into quarters, then slice into ½-inch pieces. Sauté sausage in small skillet over medium-high heat until heated through. Blot excess grease with paper towels; add sausage to soup. Makes 8 to 10 servings.

WEDDING SOUP

One Day Ahead: Stew whole chicken in stock pot with 1 onion, 1 carrot and 1 rib of celery. When chicken is cooked, strain stock and debone chicken. Save 2 cups chicken for soup. Refrigerate stock overnight and remove fat from surface.

For Soup:

1 diced onion
2 cloves garlic
1 finely diced carrot
1 lb. ground beef
½ c. Parmesan cheese

¼ c. bread crumbs
1 c. dry acini de pepe or
   other small pasta
2 c. diced escarole

Soften onion, garlic and carrot in olive oil in large pot. Add stock and bring to boil. Season to taste with salt and pepper. Make small meatballs with beef, cheese and bread crumbs and drop into boiling stock. Add dry pasta and chicken. Reduce heat and add escarole. Simmer ½ hour.

Janey Morell

❧ CHEESEBURGER SOUP ❧

½ lb. ground beef
¾ c. chopped onion
¾ c. shredded carrots
¾ c. diced celery
1 tsp. dried basil
1 tsp. dried parsley flakes
4 Tbsp. butter or margarine,
   divided
3 c. chicken broth

4 c. diced peeled potatoes
   (1 ¾ lb.)
¼ c. all-purpose flour
8 oz. process American
   cheese, cubed (2 c.)
1 ½ c. milk
¾ tsp. salt
¼ to ½ tsp. pepper
¼ c. sour cream

In a 3-quart saucepan, brown beef; drain and set aside. In the same saucepan, saute onion, carrots, celery, basil and parsley in 1 tablespoon butter until vegetables are tender, about 10 minutes. Add broth, potatoes and beef; bring to a boil. Reduce heat; cover and simmer 10 to 12 minutes or until potatoes are tender.

Leigh Ann Gigliotti

❧ BAKED POTATO SOUP ❧

4 large baking potatoes
   (about 2 ¾ lb.)
⅔ c. butter or margarine
⅔ c. all-purpose flour
¾ tsp. salt
¼ tsp. white pepper
6 c. milk

1 c. (8 oz.) sour cream
¼ c. thinly sliced green
   onions
10 bacon strips, cooked and
   crumbled
1 c. (4 oz.) shredded Cheddar
   cheese

Bake potatoes at 350° for 65 to 75 minutes or until tender; cool completely. Peel and cube potatoes. In a large saucepan, melt butter; stir in flour, salt and pepper until smooth. Gradually add milk. Bring to a boil; cook and stir for 2 minutes or until thickened. Remove from the heat; whisk in sour cream. Add potatoes and green onions. Garnish with bacon and cheese. Yield: 10 servings.

Leigh Ann Gigliotti

BROCCOLI-MUSHROOM SOUP

1 small onion
1 stick oleo
1 lb. fresh mushrooms, cut up
1 bunch broccoli, cut up
1 Tbsp. Worcestershire sauce
1 tsp. garlic salt
pepper to taste
3 cans cream of mushroom soup
2 cans milk
¾ c. small curd cottage cheese

Sauté onion and oleo. Add mushrooms, broccoli, Worcestershire sauce, garlic salt and pepper to taste. Cook 35 to 40 minutes or until tender. In large saucepan (8-quart), combine cream of mushroom soup, milk and cottage cheese. Add cooked vegetables to soup mixture and serve.

Kathy Lore

BROCCOLI AND CHEESE SOUP

2 Tbsp. finely chopped onion
3 Tbsp. flour
dash of pepper
1 c. shredded sharp Cheddar cheese
1 ½ c. water
2 Tbsp. butter
½ tsp. salt
2 c. milk
2 chicken bouillon cubes
1 (10 oz.) pkg. frozen broccoli

Cook onion in butter until tender. Stir in flour, salt and pepper. Add milk and cheese, stirring constantly, until cheese is melted. Remove from heat. Bring water to boil in separate pan and add bouillon cubes. Add frozen broccoli and cook to package directions. Do not drain. Add broccoli and liquid to cheese. Mix well.

Note: Cauliflower may be used. Add 1 tablespoon parsley flakes.

Kathy Lore

❧ STUFFED PEPPER SOUP ❧

4 lb. ground beef
2 (28 oz.) tomato sauce
2 (28 oz.) chopped tomatoes
(do not drain)
4 c. cooked long grain white
rice

6 c. chopped green peppers
4 beef bouillon cubes
¾ c. brown sugar
4 tsp. salt (optional)
2 tsp. pepper

Brown and drain beef; add remaining ingredients. Boil; reduce heat and simmer 30 to 40 minutes, until peppers are tender.

Kathy Lore

❧ FRUIT SALAD ❧

1 (3 c.) container small curd
cottage cheese
2 ⅓ c. dry apricot jello
1 (11 oz.) can crushed
pineapple, drained

2 (7 oz.) cans Mandarin
oranges, drained
1 (9 oz.) Cool Whip

Mix dry jello with cottage cheese until dissolved. Add pineapple and oranges. Fold in Cool Whip. Refrigerate.

Audrey Evans

❧ AUNT TOMMY'S GREEK SAUCE ❧

1 lb. ground beef
1 tsp. cayenne pepper
powder (may substitute 1
to 2 tsp. Red Hot sauce)
1 tsp. basil
1 tsp. garlic salt
2 medium onions, diced
small

1 ½ c. water
1 tsp. salt
1 tsp. red pepper flakes
1 tsp. oregano
1 tsp. chili powder
1 tsp. cumin powder
2 ½ c. tomato sauce
1 Tbsp. mustard

Fry ground beef and drain. Combine all ingredients into large saucepan and simmer for 1 ½ to 2 hours. Add spices to taste. Best taste after sitting for a day and reheating. Serve over hot dogs, sausages, hamburgers, etc.

In Memory of Thomas Kindle

❦ ROSAMARINA ❦

¾ c. sugar
½ tsp. salt (optional)
1 large egg
2 Tbsp. flour
2 cans medium pineapple (14 oz. I think) or whatever canned fruit you want*

2 cans medium (14 oz. I think) mandarin oranges
1 jar maraschino cherries
1 box rosamarina (16 oz.)
2 (10 oz.) Cool Whip

*I like raspberry flavored peaches, fruit cocktail, etc.; the canned peaches were like 99 cents to $1.19 a can if that helps on the size.

Drain pineapple chunks (or whatever fruit you choose) and mandarin oranges, saving the juice for the sauce and saving the fruit for later (if you get the peaches or any large-cut fruit, make sure you cut them up into smaller pieces and the oranges, too).

Sauce: Mix sugar, salt, egg, fruit juice, mandarin orange juice and flour over medium heat. Bring to boil and cook to custard consistency, stirring occasionally to prevents burning. Remove from heat and cool thoroughly. Cook rosamarina 8 minutes +/-. Cool. When sufficiently cooled, fold rosamarina into cooled sauce mixture. Refrigerate overnight.

Next morning, fold in fruit (pineapple, mandarin oranges, cherries, etc.). Then fold in Cool Whip (usually 1 ½ tubs of Cool Whip). The rosamarina will soak up the Cool Whip so keep the last ½ tub to refresh the rosamarina when needed. You can use the strawberry Cool Whip, too, if you want; my girlfriend said it tasted great!

When serving, I usually put 2 pineapple slices across the top of the rosamarina dish and put 2 cherries in the middle of the pineapple center. Pretty.

Kathy Maughn

SOUPS, SALADS & SAUCES

🌿 LINGUINE TUNA SALAD 🌿

(Makes 6 servings.)

1 (7 oz.) pkg. linguine or whatever pasta you choose
¼ c. ReaLemon lemon juice
¼ c. vegetable oil
2 tsp. sugar
¼ c. sliced green onions (optional)
1 tsp. Italian seasoning
1 tsp. seasoned salt
½ tsp. Tabasco pepper sauce or Red Hot sauce (optional)
1 (12 ½ oz.) can Star Kist tuna, drained
1 (10 oz.) pkg. frozen green peas, thawed (I use mixed vegetables instead)
2 medium tomatoes, chopped

Cook linguine (pasta) according to instructions. Cook frozen vegetables according to instructions. In large bowl (use your Pampered Chef salad dressing container!), combine ReaLemon brand lemon juice, oil, onions and seasonings (sugar, seasoned salt, Italian seasoning, hot pepper sauce); mix well. Add hot linguine; toss. Add hot vegetables; toss. Add remaining ingredients (tuna fish and tomatoes); mix well. Enjoy hot or chill. Refrigerate leftovers. You can substitute chicken or shrimp for the tuna fish!!

Kathy Maughn

🌿 FRUIT SALAD 🌿

1 large vanilla pudding
2 cans pineapple (chunk)
1 can mandarin oranges
strawberries
grapes
bananas (add just before serving)
add any fruit you want

Mix pineapple juice and pudding mix. Drain all other fruits. Mix together and chill.

To reduce, use 1 small package vanilla pudding to 1 can pineapple.

Kathy Lore

🌿 BROCCOLI SALAD 🌿

6 slices bacon, crisp and crumbled
1 head broccoli, cut into small pieces
1 medium onion, chopped
1 to 1 ½ c. shredded Cheddar cheese
1 c. Miracle Whip salad dressing
½ c. sugar
2 Tbsp. vinegar

Mix Miracle Whip, sugar and vinegar. Add bacon, broccoli, onion and Cheddar cheese. Chill.

Kathy Lore

STRAWBERRY AND ROMAINE SALAD

Dressing:

2 c. mayonnaise
⅔ c. sugar
⅓ c. light cream

⅓ c. raspberry vinegar
1 Tbsp. poppy seeds
2 Tbsp. strawberry jam

Combine dressing ingredients.

romaine, washed and torn
red onion, sliced

fresh strawberries, sliced
slivered almonds

Toss romaine, onion and strawberries. Just before serving, add dressing to taste. This dressing can be refrigerated at least a week.

Carol Eckert

RAMEN NOODLE SALAD

1 (16 oz.) pkg. coleslaw or
   broccoli
1 c. toasted almonds*
2 pkg. chicken Ramen
   noodle soup
½ c. sugar

1 large onion*
1 c. sunflower seeds*
1 ¼ c. oil
⅓ c. white vinegar
splash of garlic powder and
   pepper*

Crumble noodles; mix with cole slaw. Combine oil, sugar, vinegar and seasoning packet (from Ramen noodles). Pour over cole slaw. Refrigerate 8 hours. Add nuts and sunflower seeds just before serving.

*Optional. Don't need to add if you don't want to.

GREEK CONEY ISLAND SAUCE

1 lb. ground beef
2 tsp. chili powder
2 tsp. cumin powder
3 tsp. paprika
1 Tbsp. minced onions or
   more

1 tsp. oregano
½ tsp. red pepper
1 tsp. salt
¼ tsp. black pepper
2 c. hot water

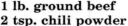

22

Cook until thick.

Great Aunt Pricilla

❧ EASY BARBECUE SAUCE ❧

1 c. ketchup	2 Tbsp. water
1 c. brown sugar	1 Tbsp. vinegar (cider)

You can add 1 tablespoon mustard, if desired. First, cook meat, then pour over meat. Bake, uncovered, in 400° oven for 15 to 20 minutes.

Betty Ann Smith

❧ GREEK SAUCE ❧

1 lb. ground beef	2 tsp. cumin
1 Tbsp. Crisco (optional)	pinch of black pepper
1 chopped onion	pinch of paprika
2 cloves garlic, crushed	1 ½ c. water
2 tsp. chili powder	

Cook onion, garlic, beef and Crisco. Add chili powder, cumin, pepper, paprika and water. Salt to taste. Cook on low until thick, approximately 1 hour. Serve over hot dogs, hamburgers or French fries (with cheese sauce). To get hamburger sauce to a smoother consistency, use an electric mixer after ingredients have cooked some.

Kathy Lore

❧ CAULIBUTTER SAUCE ❧
(For Thanksgiving)

1 head cauliflower (about 2 lb.)	2 Tbsp. instant chicken bouillon
½ c. sweet cream butter	1 Tbsp. cornstarch
¼ lb. fresh mushrooms, thinly sliced	1 c. water
⅓ c. sliced green onions	¼ tsp. Bouquet Garni (if desired)
⅓ c. slivered blanched almonds	

Wash cauliflower; separate into flowerets. In saucepan, cook cauliflower in a small amount of boiling salted water, covered, for 15 to 20 minutes or until tender. Drain. In skillet, melt butter and stir in mushrooms, onions, almonds and chicken bouillon. Saute until mushrooms are tender. Dissolve cornstarch in water; stir into butter mixture. Cook, stirring constantly, until sauce thickens. Stir in Bouquet Garni.

Louise Johnson

❧ BROCCOLI SLAW ❧

2 pkg. broccoli slaw
2 pkg. Ramen noodles
  (chicken)
½ c. sunflower seeds

3 packets chicken flavor
  seasoning
⅓ c. cider vinegar
½ c. olive oil
½ c. sugar

Put broccoli slaw, noodles and sunflower seeds in large bowl. In separate bowl, mix remaining ingredients. Take the mixture and add it to the large bowl of mixture. Put in refrigerator overnight.

Patti Sitter

❧ COLE SLAW DRESSING ❧

5 Tbsp. sugar
1 Tbsp. plus 1 tsp. flour
1 tsp. dry mustard
pinch of salt
¼ c. vinegar

¾ c. water
¼ c. butter
1 egg, beaten
1 c. Hellmann's salad
  dressing

Thoroughly mix sugar, flour, mustard, salt and egg. Combine vinegar, water and butter. Bring to a boil. Add first mixture and cook a few minutes. Remove from heat. Beat well. Add salad dressing and beat again. Will keep in refrigerator for several weeks. Also great as a vegetable dip!

Betty Ann Smith

❧ ORANGE-CUCUMBER SALAD ❧

3 oranges, peeled and sliced
1 cucumber, peeled and
  sliced
½ green bell pepper, seeded
  and cut into small pieces

¼ red onion, thinly sliced
3 Tbsp. cider vinegar
1 tsp. canola oil
1 ½ tsp. sugar
¼ tsp. salt

In medium bowl, combine the oranges, cucumbers, pepper and onion. Add the vinegar, oil, sugar and salt; toss to coat. Serve at once. Makes 4 servings.

Louise Johnson

🌿 3 BEAN SALAD 🌿

1 (No. 2) can green beans, drained
1 (No. 2) can yellow beans, drained

1 (No. 2) can kidney beans, drained

Can also add green pepper and onion to taste.

Dressing:

½ c. salad oil
¾ c. sugar

½ c. vinegar

Heat these last 3 ingredients well. Cool. Pour over beans.

🌿 RASPBERRY TOSSED SALAD 🌿

9 c. torn mixed salad greens
3 c. fresh or frozen
  unsweetened raspberries
2 Tbsp. olive or canola oil

2 Tbsp. cider vinegar
4 tsp. sugar
⅛ tsp. salt
dash of pepper

In a large salad bowl, gently combine the salad greens and 2 ¾ cups raspberries. Mash the remaining berries; strain, reserving juice and discarding seeds. In a bowl, whisk the raspberry juice, oil, vinegar, sugar, salt and pepper. Drizzle over salad; gently toss to coat. Yield: 12 servings.

Louise Johnson

🌿 THREE-BEAN SALAD 🌿

1 (16 oz.) can no salt added
  green beans, drained
1 (16 oz.) can wax beans,
  drained
1 (16 oz.) can kidney beans,
  drained
1 c. chopped green bell
  peppers

⅔ c. chopped green onions
⅔ c. apple juice
⅓ c. cider vinegar
2 tsp. sugar
½ tsp. pepper
¼ tsp. dry mustard
¼ tsp. paprika
½ tsp. dried oregano

Combine first 5 ingredients in a large bowl and toss gently. Combine apple juice and next 6 ingredients in a small jar. Cover tightly and shake well. Pour vinaigrette over salad. Toss gently. Cover and chill at least 2 hours. Makes 12 servings.

❧ SEVEN LAYER SALAD ❧

1 head lettuce, shredded
1 c. celery, diced
4 hard-boiled eggs, sliced

1 (10 oz.) pkg. frozen peas (uncooked)
1 sweet onion, chopped
½ c. green pepper (optional)

Layer in a glass 13 x 9 pan. Mix 2 cups mayo with 2 tablespoons sugar. Spread over top with diced tomatoes and 4 ounces grated Cheddar cheese. Top with diced tomatoes and ½ pound bacon.

Rita Donner

❧ PEPPER CABBAGE ❧

1 medium head cabbage, chopped fine
1 medium green pepper
1 small grated onion
1 medium carrot, grated

¼ c. sugar
1 tsp. salt
½ c. milk
⅓ c. vinegar

Blend sugar, salt, milk and vinegar and pour over and mix well.

❧ MANDARIN ORANGE SALAD ❧

Dressing:

½ tsp. salt
2 Tbsp. vinegar
2 Tbsp. sugar

¼ c. salad oil
dash of Tabasco sauce
1 Tbsp. parsley

Shake dressing and refrigerate. Melt 1 tablespoon sugar and 1 teaspoon water over low heat; add ¼ cup slivered almonds and simmer for 3 to 5 minutes. Dry on a piece of waxed paper.

mixed greens
2 green onions, sliced

1 can mandarin oranges

Put salad in a bag and refrigerate until ready to use. mix together lettuce, dressing and a can of mandarin oranges; add almonds and serve.

Linda Holman

APPLE-TURKEY SALAD

4 c. diced turkey
1 c. grapes or cherries
1 c. diced apples

1 c. pineapple tidbits
1 c. walnuts, chopped
mayonnaise (to mix well)

Serve with crackers.

Harriet Lapp

CHIFFON JELLO FRUIT SALAD

1 ½ c. well drained peach slices (canned)
1 c. very hot peach syrup or syrup and water
1 (3 oz.) pkg. lemon jello

½ c. diced celery
½ c. chopped nuts
⅓ c. mayonnaise
1 ½ c. Cool Whip

Line bottom of 1 ½-quart mold with 8 peach slices. Mix hot peach syrup and jello to dissolve jello. Chill until thickened. Add celery, nuts, mayonnaise and remaining chopped peaches. Blend. Mix with Cool Whip. Spoon into salad mold. Chill until firm (about 3 hours or more). Can unmold on lettuce.

Agnes Billisits

STRAWBERRY PRETZEL SALAD

3 Tbsp. sugar
2 c. crushed pretzels (not too fine)
¾ c. margarine, melted
½ c. powdered sugar
1 (9 oz.) carton Cool Whip

8 oz. cream cheese
2 c. mini marshmallows
6 oz. strawberry Jell-O
2 ½ boiling water
1 (16 oz.) or 2 (10 oz.) frozen strawberries

Mix the first 3 ingredients; press in a 9 x 13 pan. Bake for 15 minutes at 350°. It will look bubbly; set aside to cool. Cream powdered sugar and cream cheese. Fold in Cool Whip and marshmallows and spread over the baked layer. Dissolve Jell-O in water; stir in strawberries. Chill until slightly thickened. Decorate with more whipped topping, if desired. Good to make the day before serving.

Nancy Root

—•EXTRA RECIPES•—

Meats and Main Dishes

Recipe Favorites

Page No.
_____

Recipe Title:_____

_____

_____

_____

_____

_____

_____

_____

_____

Family Favorites

Page No.
_____

Recipe Title:_____

_____

_____

_____

_____

_____

Notes:_____

_____

_____

_____

MEATS & MAIN DISHES

🌿 CHICKEN CRESCENTS 🌿

4 chicken breasts, boiled and
  cut into small pieces
1 tsp. sage (use when
  cooking chicken)
1 (8 oz.) cream cheese,
  softened

1 can crescent dinner rolls
1 stick margarine, melted
1 bag Pepperidge Farm herb
  stuffing mix

Sauce:

1 can each cream of
  mushroom soup and cream
  of chicken soup

½ can chicken broth
½ soup can of milk

Preheat oven to 350°. Cook chicken with sage, salt and pepper. Cut in small pieces or shred. Mix chicken with cream cheese. Open rolls and mash the seams together between two pieces to create a square. Cut square into 3 strips. Place a large spoonful of chicken/cheese mixture on each strip and roll up. Dip roll in melted margarine; roll in stuffing mixture. Place on greased baking sheet and bake until lightly browned.

Mix sauce and heat in saucepan. Pour over chicken crescents when ready to serve.

Audrey Evans

🌿 TUNA PATTIES 🌿

½ c. diced red onion
2 Tbsp. dried parsley
½ tsp. onion salt and garlic
  salt
½ c. bread crumbs
2 eggs

3 cans flaked tuna (not
  albacore)
½ c. grated Parmesan cheese
½ c. shredded Cheddar
  cheese

Mix all ingredients. Form into patties approximately 3-inches wide and dredge in additional bread crumbs. Panfry in olive oil. Serve over salad with light vinaigrette or honey mustard dressing or serve on whole wheat buns. Serves 4.

Janey Morell

❧ STUFFED CABBAGE ❧

1 head cabbage

1 large can crushed tomatoes

Filling:

1 lb. ground beef
½ tsp. salt and pepper

1 c. Minute rice (uncooked)
1 egg

Cut core from cabbage and boil until leaves separate.
Mix filling and roll into cooked cabbage leaves. In large stockpot, soften 1 small onion in olive oil. Place assembled stuffed cabbage in bottom of pot. Cover with 1 can of tomatoes and 1 can of water. Cover and cook over low heat for 1 hour.

Janey Morell

❧ 15 MINUTE CHEESY CHICKEN AND RICE ❧

1 Tbsp. oil
4 chicken breasts (boneless, skinless)
1 ¾ c. water

2 c. Minute rice
2 c. broccoli flowerets
12 oz. cubed Velveeta cheese

Heat oil in medium-high heat. Add chicken breasts. Cover and cook 4 minutes. Remove from skillet. Add water; bring to boil. Stir in rice, broccoli and Velveeta cheese. Top with chicken; cover. Cook on low for 5 minutes.

Anonymous

❧ FETTUCCINE ALFREDO ❧

1 (8 oz.) pkg. cream cheese, cubed
1 c. grated Parmesan cheese
½ c. butter or margarine

½ c. milk
8 oz. fettuccine, cooked and drained

Stir cream cheese, Parmesan cheese, butter and milk in large saucepan on low heat until smooth. Add fettuccine; toss lightly. Serve with additional Parmesan cheese.

Time approximately 5 minutes. Cook time: Approximately 15 minutes. Makes 4 servings.

I use fresh grated Parmesan cheese and I add garlic to taste.

Another note: I usually pour sauce in a bowl and let family pour their desired amount on their serving.

Anonymous

❧ SEAFOOD LASAGNA ❧

lasagna noodles, cooked
½ to 1 lb. Mozzarella cheese
1 chopped onion
2 Tbsp. butter
8 oz. cream cheese
16 oz. Ricotta cheese
1 egg, beaten
2 tsp. dry basil
½ tsp. salt

¼ tsp. pepper
2 cans mushroom soup
⅓ c. milk
⅓ c. white wine
2 lb. or more seafood
  (shrimp, scallops, fish, crab
  meat, lobster or a
  combination)
¼ to ½ c. Parmesan cheese

May add mushrooms.

Saute onion in butter. Mix cream cheese, Ricotta cheese, egg, basil, salt and pepper with onion mix. Mix together remaining ingredients in a bowl. Place one layer of noodles in 9 x 13 pan. Spread with ⅓ Ricotta mix. Top with ⅓ soup-seafood mix. Sprinkle with Mozzarella cheese. Repeat layers x two. Bake 1 hour and 30 minutes at 325°. Let stand 10 minutes before serving.

Harriet Lapp

❧ MICROWAVE FISH ❧

1 lb. fish
3 Tbsp. margarine
3 Tbsp. soy sauce
2 Tbsp. orange juice
  concentrate or pineapple
  juice concentrate

dash of each garlic salt and
  pepper
salt

Defrost fish (1 pound = 7 to 9 minutes).

Melt margarine. Add soy sauce, orange juice or pineapple juice, garlic salt and pepper. Sprinkle with salt. Cook, covered, until fish flakes; turn. Cook approximately 7 to 10 minutes. Sprinkle fish with ¼ teaspoon grated orange peel to serve.

❧ SIRLOIN TIPS ❧

1 can cream of mushroom
  soup
1 can French onion soup

½ c. red wine (optional)
2 Tbsp. Worcestershire sauce

Mix together. Add 2 pounds of sirloin tip roast (cubed). Bake, covered, at 350° for 2 ½ to 3 hours or put in a crock-pot. Serve over noodles.

Linda Holman

❧ QUICK CHEESEBURGER ❧

1 lb. ground beef
¾ c. chopped onion
1 can Cheddar cheese soup
1 c. frozen mixed vegetables

¼ c. milk
2 c. Bisquick baking mix
¾ c. water
1 c. shredded cheese

Brown ground beef and chopped onion together. Then stir in cheese soup, milk and mixed vegetables. In a separate bowl, mix Bisquick and water. Spread Bisquick batter evenly into a greased 13 x 9 baking pan. Spread ground beef and vegetable mixture over batter. Sprinkle with Cheddar cheese. Bake 30 minutes at 375° to 400°, depending on your oven.

Rita Donner

❧ EASY SWEET AND SOUR PORK ❧

1 ½ to 2 lb. boneless sliced
  lean shoulder pork
2 Tbsp. shortening
1 can pineapple chunks
¾ c. water
¼ c. vinegar
1 Tbsp. soy sauce

¼ c. brown sugar
½ tsp. salt
2 Tbsp. cornstarch
2 Tbsp. water
⅓ c. thinly sliced onion
¾ c. thinly sliced green
  pepper

Cut meat into strips 3 to 4-inches long and 1-inch wide. Melt shortening in skillet; cook meat until lightly browned. Drain pineapple and mix juice, water, vinegar, soy sauce, brown sugar and salt. Pour over meat. Cover and simmer 1 hour, until tender. Combine cornstarch and 2 tablespoons of water. Add to meat and cook over low heat, stirring constantly, until thickened. Add pineapple chunks, onion and green pepper. Cover and simmer 10 to 15 minutes, until vegetables are tender. Serve on rice. Yield: 4 to 6 servings.

Rita Donner

❧ SPICY PORK CHOPS ❧
(Can broil or cook on grill.)

⅓ c. soy sauce	1 tsp. ginger
¼ c. sugar	

Mix together. Brush with sauce as they cook.

Barbara Fehr

❧ TEXAS TWO STEP CHICKEN ❧

1 ½ c. salsa	1 Tbsp. Dijon mustard
3 Tbsp. brown sugar	boneless chicken

Place chicken in 2-quart shallow baking dish. Pour sauce mixture over chicken. Bake at 400° for 20 minutes. Serve over cooked rice.

Sally Buck

❧ STUFFED PEPPERS ❧

1 lb. ground beef	2 (10 ¾ oz.) cans tomato soup
¾ c. white rice	2 medium green peppers

Mix by hand beef, rice and 2 tablespoons condensed soup; save the rest of the can. Clean and halve each pepper. Split beef evenly into each of the 4 pepper halves. Mix remaining soup with water as can directs. Place peppers in baking dish. Pour soup over peppers until dish is full; there may be a little extra soup. Cover dish with foil and bake at 375° for about an hour (until peppers are soft).

My mom likes to cook the last 15 minutes with the foil off; this is personal preference.

Kaitlin Ames

❧ QUICK LASAGNA ❧

1 lb. ground beef
½ c. Miracle Whip
½ c. Parmesan cheese
6 lasagna noodles, cooked

1 jar spaghetti sauce
2 c. (8 oz.) shredded
   Mozzarella

Brown and drain ground beef, then stir in dressing and Parmesan cheese. Layer ½ of noodles and meat mixture, sauce and cheese in 12 x 8 baking dish. Repeat layers. Bake at 350° for 30 minutes. Makes 6 to 8 servings.

Barbara Fehr

❧ SURPRISE HAMBURGS ❧

1 ½ lb. hamburg
1 c. oatmeal
1 Tbsp. chopped onions

1 tsp. each salt and pepper
1 c. milk

Mix and fry like regular hamburgs. Put in casserole and cover with sauce. Bake in oven for 1 hour at 350°.

Sauce:

1 c. catsup
3 Tbsp. vinegar
2 Tbsp. Worcestershire sauce

1 Tbsp. sugar
½ c. water

Audrey Evans

❧ QUICK CHICKEN QUESADILLAS ❧

Prep Time: 25 minutes. Start to Finish: 25 minutes. Makes 4 quesadillas.

6 oz. refrigerated cooked
   Southwest-flavor chicken
   breast strips (from 9 or 12
   oz. pkg.)
½ c. Old El Paso® thick 'n
   chunky salsa

1 (11.5 oz.) pkg. Old El Paso®
   flour tortillas for burritos
   (eight 8-inch tortillas)
cooking spray
2 c. finely shredded
   Colby-Monterey Jack
   cheese blend (8 oz.)
¼ c. sour cream

Cut chicken into bite-size pieces. In small bowl, mix chicken and salsa. Spray 1 side of 1 tortilla with cooking spray; place sprayed side down in 10-inch nonstick skillet. Layer with ¼ of the chicken mixture and ½ cup of the cheese. Top with another tortilla; spray top of tortilla with cooking spray. Cook, uncovered, over medium heat 4 to 6 minutes, carefully turning after 2 minutes, until golden brown. Repeat with remaining tortillas, chicken mixture and cheese. To serve, cut quesadillas into wedges. Serve with sour cream and, if desired, additional salsa.

Lee Ann Arble

❧ BIG BATCH CHEESEBURGER ❧ BAKE

Prep Time: 20 minutes. Makes 16 to 20 servings.

1 ½ lb. (at least 80%) ground beef
1 ¼ c. chopped onions (about 2 large)
1 (10 ¾ oz.) can condensed Cheddar cheese soup
1 ¼ c. Green Giant® frozen mixed vegetables (if desired)

½ c. milk
2 ⅓ c. original Bisquick® mix
⅔ c. water
1 ⅓ c. shredded Cheddar cheese (about 5 oz.)

Heat oven to 375°. Generously spray bottom and sides of 15 x 10 x 1-inch pan with cooking spray. In 12-inch skillet, cook beef and onions over medium heat, stirring occasionally, until beef is thoroughly cooked; drain. Stir in soup, vegetables and milk. In large bowl, stir Bisquick mix and water until moistened. Spread evenly in pan. Spread beef mixture over batter. Sprinkle with cheese. Bake, uncovered, 35 minutes.

Lee Ann Arble

❧ IMPOSSIBLE EASY CHICKEN POT ❧ PIE

Prep Time: 5 minutes. Start to Finish: 35 minutes. Makes 6 servings.

1 ⅔ c. Green Giant® frozen
mixed vegetables
1 c. cut up cooked chicken
1 (10 ¾ oz.) can condensed
cream of chicken soup

1 c. original Bisquick® mix
½ c. milk
1 egg

Heat oven to 400°. Mix vegetables, chicken and soup in ungreased glass pie plate, 9 x 1 ¼-inches. Stir together remaining ingredients with fork until blended. Pour into pie plate. Bake 30 minutes or until golden brown.

High Altitude (3500 to 6500 feet): Heat oven to 425°.

Lee Ann Arble

❧ TUSCAN CHICKEN PASTA ❧

1 lb. boneless, skinless
chicken breasts, cut into
1-inch pieces
1 (15 ½ oz.) can red kidney
beans, rinsed and drained
1 (15 oz.) can tomato sauce
2 (14 ½ oz.) cans Italian-style
stewed tomatoes (diced
tomatoes or fresh tomatoes
work well, also)
1 (4 ½ oz.) jar sliced
mushrooms, drained or 1 c.
fresh mushrooms

1 medium green bell pepper,
chopped
½ c. onion, chopped
½ c. celery, chopped
4 cloves garlic, minced
1 c. water
1 tsp. dried Italian seasoning
(Mrs. Dash tomato, basil,
garlic seasoning blend)
6 oz. uncooked thin
spaghetti, broken in half

Place all ingredients EXCEPT spaghetti in slow cooker (crock-pot). Cover and cook on low 4 hours or until vegetables are tender. Turn to high. Stir in spaghetti; cover. Stir again after 10 minutes. Cover and cook 30 to 45 minutes or until pasta is tender. Makes 8 servings.

❧ HAM LOAF ❧

1 lb. lean ground ham
1 lb. lean ground pork
1 c. Wheaties
2 eggs, beaten

1 c. canned milk
1 tsp. salt
1 tsp. pepper

Mix all ingredients together. Pack well into an 8 ½ x 1 ½ x 2 ½-inch loaf pan. Pull meat away from side of pan with a scraper. Bake at 350° for 30 minutes, then bake at

250° for another 1 ½ hours, basting occasionally with the following sauce.

Sauce:

½ c. warm water
¼ c. vinegar
½ c. brown sugar

¼ c. Worcestershire
1 tsp. dry mustard

Mix this together in a saucepan and bring to a boil; baste.

Rita Donner

❧ HAM LOAF ❧
(Serves 8.)

2 eggs
1 c. milk
1 c. dry bread crumbs
¼ tsp. pepper

1 ½ lb. ground fully cooked
   ham
½ lb. ground pork

Glaze:

⅓ c. brown sugar
¼ c. vinegar

½ tsp. ground mustard
2 Tbsp. water

Beat eggs. Add milk, bread crumbs and pepper. Add ham and pork; mix well. Shape into loaf. Bake in shallow pan. Bake at 350° for 30 minutes.

Meanwhile, combine glaze ingredients. Spoon over loaf. Continue baking 40 minutes longer or until a meat thermometer reaches 170°, basting occasionally with glaze.

❧ POOR MAN'S STEW ❧

1 lb. ground meat
1 can peas
1 can sliced carrots

1 can cream-style corn
mashed potatoes

Cook and drain ground meat. In a baking dish, line the bottom with the ground meat. Add drained can of peas, drained can of carrots and can of cream-style corn. Cover with leftover mashed potatoes or instant mashed potatoes, made according to package. Heat in 350° oven for ½ hour. Can be made ahead of time and refrigerated. Cooking time will be longer. Can cover potatoes with shredded cheese.

Wilma Kenny

SLOW COOKER CHICKEN STEW

2 onions, chopped
2 chicken breasts, cubed
1 lb. baby carrots
6 medium potatoes, cubed

4 oz. can sliced mushrooms
(undrained)
2 cans cream of mushroom
soup

Combine all ingredients in slow cooker. Cook on high for 2 hours; reduce to low for 5 to 6 hours.

Helen McKenzie

TURKEY CUTLETS WITH CRANBERRY-PEAR CHUTNEY

(Serves 4; 5 Weight Watchers Points.)

6 Tbsp. packed light brown
sugar
¼ c. chicken broth
¼ c. apple cider vinegar
2 Tbsp. orange juice
¼ tsp. cinnamon
¼ tsp. ground ginger
pinch of ground cloves
4 (¼ lb.) turkey cutlets

½ tsp. salt
¼ tsp. coarsely ground black
pepper
1 tsp. canola oil
1 ripe pear, peeled and
chopped or 2 canned pear
halves
1 c. fresh or frozen
cranberries

Whisk together brown sugar, chicken broth, vinegar, orange juice, cinnamon, ground ginger and cloves in small bowl and set aside. Sprinkle cutlets with salt and pepper. Heat oil in large nonstick skillet over medium-high heat. Add cutlets and cook approximately 3 minutes on a side until done. Transfer to plate to keep warm.

Add pear, cranberries and sugar mixture to skillet; bring to a boil. Simmer, uncovered, until berries pop and chutney thickens, 5 to 7 minutes. Spoon chutney over cutlets. Good with noodles.

Gail Sollman

BBQ BEEF CUPS

1 lb. ground beef
½ c. BBQ sauce
1 Tbsp. diced onion

1 ½ tsp. brown sugar
¾ c. shredded Cheddar
1 tube refrigerated biscuits

Brown meat and drain. Stir in sauce, onion and brown sugar. Place each biscuit in a muffin tin. Make a hole; spoon in meat mixture. Top with cheese. Bake at 400° for 10 to 12 minutes.

Gail Sollman

❧ APRICOT CHICKEN ❧

1 bottle French dressing
1 jar apricot preserves

1 pkg. Lipton onion soup mix
4 to 6 chicken breasts

Mix and pour over uncooked chicken breast. Bake at 350° for 1 hour. (So fast to make if you have unexpected company!) Serve over cooked rice. You'll get nothing but compliments.

Gloria Love

❧ ELEPHANT STEW ❧

1 elephant
2 rabbits

salt
pepper

Cut elephant into small bite-sized pieces. Add enough brown gravy to cover. Cook in pan on stove about 465° (takes about 3 weeks). this will serve 3800. If more are expected, add 2 rabbits, but do this only if necessary as most people don't like hare in their stew!!

Gloria Love

❧ FOOTBALL STEW ❧

5 medium carrots
5 potatoes
1 can tomato soup
1 can cream mushroom soup

1 pkg. dry onion soup mix
1 c. red wine
2 lb. beef, cut into 1-inch cubes

Cut and peel carrots and potatoes. Put into small roaster. Add soups and wine; mix. Bake at 275° for 4 or 5 hours (stir occasionally), covered. Serve.

Karen Souder

❧ CREAMED CHIPPED BEEF ❧

3 Tbsp. butter
3 Tbsp. onion, chopped
3 Tbsp. green pepper, chopped
3 Tbsp. flour
2 c. milk

1 Tbsp. parsley or chives
2 Tbsp. dry sherry
8 oz. chipped beef, finely chopped (scissors work well)

Melt butter. Saute onion and green pepper. Sprinkle in flour. Add remaining ingredients.

Karen Souders

CREAMED CABBAGE AND DRIED BEEF

½ large head cabbage
⅛ lb. dried beef

1 ½ c. Medium White Sauce
½ c. buttered bread crumbs

Cook coarsely chopped cabbage in saltwater until tender. Drain. Soak chopped dried beef in ½ cup warm water for 10 minutes. Place cabbage and dried beef in alternate layers in a greased casserole dish. Pour white sauce over mixture and top with buttered crumbs. Bake at 350° for 25 minutes.

Medium White Sauce:

2 Tbsp. margarine
2 Tbsp. flour

¼ tsp. salt
1 c. milk

Melt margarine in saucepan over low heat. Blend flour, salt and dash of white pepper. Add to margarine and add milk slowly. Cook until thickened.

Audrey Evans

BRUNSWICK STEW

1 ½ lb. lean stew beef
2 ½ lb. chicken pieces
1 ½ lb. lean pork
6 c. chopped tomatoes
4 c. chopped potatoes
2 c. butter beans
2 c. corn

1 c. finely chopped onion
¼ c. catsup
¼ c. vinegar
2 Tbsp. Worcestershire sauce
1 Tbsp. sugar
salt and cayenne pepper to
    taste

Cook beef, chicken and pork in water to cover in saucepan until tender. Drain saucepan, reserving broth. Cool and shred meat. Cook tomatoes, potatoes, beans, corn and onion in reserved broth in saucepan until tender. Add meat, catsup, vinegar, Worcestershire sauce, sugar and salt and cayenne pepper. Simmer for 1 ½ hours or to desired consistency.

Chill for several days and reheat for best flavor. May substitute canned vegetables for fresh, if preferred. Yield: 16 servings.

Audrey Evans

❧ SOUR CREAM ENCHILADAS ❧

Bake, covered, at 350° for 1 hour. Uncover last 10 minutes.

12 flour tortillas	1 medium onion, chopped
2 lb. ground beef	2 stalks celery, chopped

Cook together ground beef, onion and celery until meat is done.

Sauce:

2 cans cream of chicken soup	1 pt. sour cream
½ c. chopped green chiles	1 c. milk
	¾ Cheddar cheese

Put 2 generous tablespoons meat mixture on each tortilla. Roll up and place in lightly oiled pan or dish.

Mix sauce ingredients and pour over enchiladas. Serves 6 to 8.

Karen Souder

❧ TACOS IN A BAG ❧

Great for casual dinner parties; no dishes to wash! Kids love this!!

4 small bags Doritos nacho cheese tortilla chips (about 1 ¾ oz.), slightly crushed in the bag*

Cut one long side open (turn outside of bag up). Layer each bag on chips: ⅓ cup Sloppy Joe meat (hot), ⅓ cup chopped lettuce, ⅓ cup diced tomatoes and ⅓ cup grated Cheddar cheese. Top with 2 tablespoons of sour cream. Hand each person a plastic fork and it's ready to eat!

*Or get large bag of Doritos nacho cheese tortilla chips and crush in quart size plastic bags.

Gloria Love

SAUCY COCKTAIL MEAT BALLS

1 lb. ground beef
2 Tbsp. bread crumbs
1 egg, beaten
½ tsp. salt
½ c. chopped onions and
    green peppers

2 Tbsp. butter
1 can tomato soup
2 Tbsp. brown sugar
4 tsp. Worcestershire sauce
1 Tbsp. mustard
1 Tbsp. vinegar

Mix beef, bread crumbs, eggs and salt. Make meatballs (small). Broil meatballs until brown. Cook peppers and onion in butter. Stir in rest of ingredients. Pour over meatballs. Bake at 350° for 20 minutes.

Phyllis Pierce

TACO STEW

This is really tasty and quick to make. If you don't like it spicy, use the original V-8 juice, not the spicy hot.

1 lb. ground beef
1 c. onion, diced
1 (15 oz.) can whole kernel
    corn, drained
1 (11.5 oz.) can V-8 vegetable
    juice (spicy hot or regular)
1 (15 oz.) can Ranch Style
    beans

1 (10 oz.) can Ro-Tel
    tomatoes (diced tomatoes
    and green chilies)
1 (1 ¼ oz.) envelope taco
    seasoning mix
1 c. water
tortilla chips
Cheddar cheese, shredded
sour cream (optional)

In a large saucepan, cook ground beef and onion. Drain off fat. Stir in next 6 ingredients. Bring to a boil. Reduce heat and simmer, uncovered, about 20 minutes. Serve in individual bowls with Cheddar cheese and tortilla chips sprinkled on top. A dollop of sour cream, if desired.

Betty Ann Smith

CROCK-POT LASAGNA

1 lb. ground beef
1 large onion, chopped
2 garlic gloves, minced
1 (29 oz.) can tomato sauce
1 c. water
1 (6 oz.) can tomato paste
1 tsp. salt
1 tsp. dried oregano

1 (8 oz.) pkg. no-cook
    lasagna noodles
4 c. (16 oz.) shredded
    Mozzarella cheese
1 ½ c. (12 oz.) small-curd
    cottage cheese
½ c. grated Parmesan cheese

In a skillet, cook beef, onion and garlic over medium heat until meat is no longer pink; drain. Add the tomato sauce, water, tomato paste, salt and oregano; mix well. Spread ¼ of the meat sauce in an ungreased 5-quart slow cooker. Arrange ⅓ of the noodles over sauce (break the noodles if necessary). Combine the cheeses; spoon ⅓ of the mixture over noodles. Repeat layers twice. Top with remaining meat sauce. Cover and cook on low for 4 to 5 hours or until noodles are tender. (Yield: 6 to 8 servings.)

Betty Ann Smith

❧ CHICKEN A LA KING ❧

½ c. chopped onion
¼ c. chopped green pepper
¼ c. butter or margarine
2 cans (10 oz.) condensed
    cream of celery soup

1 to 1 ⅓ c. light cream
2 c. cubed cooked chicken
¼ c. diced pimento
dash of red pepper

Saute onion and green peppers in butter until tender. Blend in soup and light cream; stir until smooth. Add chicken, pimento and pepper. Stir over moderate heat until hot.

Louise Johnson

❧ BELLA BRAISED CHICKEN ❧

1 Tbsp. unsalted stick
    margarine
2 onions, chopped
2 celery stalks, diced
1 carrot, diced
2 garlic cloves, minced
3 Tbsp. all-purpose flour
¼ tsp. freshly ground black
    pepper
6 (4 oz.) skinless boneless
    chicken breasts

1 Tbsp. olive oil
1 (14 ½ oz.) can diced
    tomatoes (no salt added)
1 c. low sodium chicken
    broth
½ c. dry white wine
2 Tbsp. minced parsley plus
    more for garnish
1 tsp. dried thyme leaves

Preheat the oven to 325°. In a large nonstick skillet, melt the margarine. Add the onions, celery, carrot and garlic; cook, stirring as needed, until softened, about 5 minutes. Transfer the vegetables to a 3-quart Dutch oven or casserole. In a gallon-size sealable plastic bag, combine the flour and pepper. Add the chicken; shake to coat. In the same skillet, heat the oil. Add the chicken and brown 2 minutes on each side. Arrange the chicken on top of the vegetables. Return the skillet to the heat; add the tomatoes, broth, wine, parsley and thyme. Cook, scraping up the browned bits from the bottom of the skillet, until the liquid comes to a boil; pour over the chicken. Bake, covered, until the chicken is cooked through and the vegetables are tender, about 1 hour. Serve, sprinkled with additional minced parsley.

Jim and Rita Donner's favorite.

Louise Johnson

PICANTE CHICKEN

4 boneless, skinless chicken breast halves (1 lb.)	3 Tbsp. brown sugar
1 (16 oz.) jar picante sauce	1 Tbsp. prepared mustard
	hot cooked rice (optional)

Place chicken in a greased shallow 2-quart baking dish. In a small bowl, combine the picante sauce, brown sugar and mustard; pour over chicken. Bake, uncovered, at 400° for 30 to 35 minutes or until chicken juices run clear. Serve over rice, if desired. Yield: 4 servings.

Louise Johnson

BEEF STROGANOFF

1 lb. ground beef	1 tsp. garlic salt or 1 garlic clove
1 medium onion or ½ c. chopped	1 c. sour cream
¼ c. butter	1 (10 ½ oz.) can cream of chicken soup
2 Tbsp. flour	2 (4 oz.) cans mushrooms
1 tsp. salt	2 c. cooked noodles or rice (hot)
½ tsp. pepper	

In large skillet, add onions, meat and butter. Cook until tender. Stir in garlic, salt, flour, pepper and mushrooms. Cook 5 minutes, stirring constantly. Stir in soup. Simmer 10 minutes, uncovered. Stir in sour cream; heat through and serve over noodles or rice.

Kathy Lore

❧ BEEF STROGANOFF ❧

1 lb. ground beef
1 medium onion or ½ c.,
  chopped
¼ c. butter
2 Tbsp. flour
1 tsp. salt
½ tsp. pepper

1 tsp. garlic salt or 1 garlic
  clove
1 c. sour cream
1 (10 ½ oz.) can cream of
  chicken soup
2 (4 oz.) cans mushrooms
2 c. cooked noodles or rice
  (hot)

In large skillet, add onions, meat and butter. Cook until tender. Stir in garlic, salt, flour, pepper and mushrooms. Cook 5 minutes, stirring constantly. Stir in soup. Simmer 10 minutes, uncovered. Stir in sour cream. Heat through and serve over noodles or rice.

Kathy Lore

❧ CHEESY TUNA NOODLE ❧

2 Tbsp. butter
2 Tbsp. flour
1 c. milk
1 c. shredded Cheddar
  cheese

2 cans albacore tuna
1 small bag frozen peas
1 lb. cooked egg noodles

Make a roux with butter and flour, slowly adding milk. Season with 1 teaspoon salt and ½ teaspoon pepper. Stir in cheese until melted. Add albacore and peas and heat through. Mix in cooked egg noodles or serve over egg noodles. Serves 6.

Janey Morell

❧ ORANGE CHICKEN AND RICE ❧

1 (2 ½ to 3 lb.) ready to cook
  broiler-fryer chicken, cut
  up
¼ c. frozen orange juice
  concentrate, thawed

2 Tbsp. butter
⅓ tsp. ground ginger
Raisin Rice (recipe follows)

Preheat oven to 375°. Sprinkle chicken with salt and pepper. Place chicken pieces, skin side up and not touching, in a foil-lined shallow baking pan. Bake at 375° for 40 minutes.

In saucepan, combine cornstarch, butter and ginger; heat. Spoon this mixture over chicken and bake 20 minutes longer or until tender. Stir pan drippings to blend. Serve over Raisin Rice.

Michelle Wobrak

RAISIN RICE

1 c. water
1 Tbsp. frozen orange juice
   concentrate, thawed
1 c. packaged instant rice

2 Tbsp. raisins
½ tsp. salt
2 Tbsp. toasted slivered
   blanched almonds

In saucepan, combine water and orange juice. Bring to boil. Add rice, raisins and salt. Continue cooking according to directions on rice package. Sprinkle with almonds.

Michelle Wobrak

CHICKEN PAPRIKASH

2 tsp. olive oil
4 skinless boneless chicken
   breasts (3 oz. each)
¼ tsp. salt
¼ tsp. freshly ground pepper
1 c. chopped scallions
1 c. chopped red bell pepper

2 garlic cloves, minced
1 Tbsp. paprika
½ tsp. dried thyme
1 c. low sodium fat-free
   chicken broth
½ c. light sour cream
2 c. hot cooked white rice

In large skillet, heat oil. Sprinkle chicken with salt and pepper. Cook 3 to 4 minutes on each side until golden and cooked through. Remove from skillet; keep warm. Add scallions, bell pepper and garlic to skillet. Cook, stirring frequently, 4 to 5 minutes, until tender. Stir in paprika and thyme. Cook 1 minute longer. Stir in broth. Bring to a boil. Reduce heat to low; simmer 5 minutes, until reduced by half. Stir in sour cream; simmer 1 to 2 minutes, until heated through. To serve, arrange chicken on top of rice. Spoon sauce evenly over chicken.

Michelle Wobrak

BBQ HAMBURGER

1 lb. hamburger
1 large onion
1 Tbsp. vinegar
½ tsp. celery seed
3 Tbsp. sugar

¾ c. catsup
2 Tbsp. Worcestershire sauce
½ tsp. salt
½ tsp. mustard

Fry hamburger and onion until done; drain fat. Add remaining ingredients. Simmer for 15 to 30 minutes.

❧ BREAKFAST EGG CASSEROLE ❧

6 eggs
2 lb. sausage, cooked and
   drained
2 c. milk

6 bread slices, cubed
1 c. cheese
ham, green pepper, onion
   (optional)

Lynn Delio

❧ BEEF ZUCCHINI CASSEROLE ❧
(Really Good!!)

1 lb. ground meat
8 oz. can tomato sauce
1 tsp. salt
½ tsp. sugar
1 tsp. Worcestershire sauce
¼ tsp. hot sauce

2 small onions, chopped
1 lb. zucchini, sliced thin
4 oz. cream cheese
8 oz. sour cream
Parmesan cheese
paprika

Brown meat and onion in large skillet. Add tomato sauce, salt, sugar, Worcestershire sauce and hot sauce; cook 5 minutes. Grease 10 x 6 x 2-inch baking dish. Layer ½ of the meat, then zucchini; repeat. Combine sour cream and cream cheese, mixing well. Spread over zucchini. Sprinkle Parmesan and paprika over top. Bake at 350° for 35 minutes.

Louise Johnson

❧ NOODLE DISH ❧

noodles
1 lb. ground meat
grated onion

salt and pepper
1 can mushroom soup
¾ can of water

Cook noodles. Grate onion. Brown meat and onion. Add the meat to cooked noodles in buttered casserole. Add soup and water. Cover. Bake at 375° for 45 minutes. Can be topped with croutons.

Eileen Freeman

MAC SAUSAGE AND BROCCOLI BAKE

1 (7 ¼ oz.) macaroni and
  cheese dinner
1 (10 oz.) pkg. frozen
  broccoli spears, thawed
  and drained
1 lb. smoked sausage, cut
  into ½-inch pieces
1 can cream of celery soup
¼ c. green onion slices

Prepare dinner (package directions). Cut broccoli into 1-inch pieces. Add with remaining ingredients to dinner. Mix well. Put in 2-quart casserole and bake at 350° for 45 minutes. Makes 6 to 8 servings.

Barbara Fehr

CHICKEN CASSEROLE

boneless chicken, cooked
  and cut into pieces
1 pkg. frozen mixed
  vegetables
1 can creamed chicken soup
1 pkg. frozen potato puffs

Mix chicken, vegetables and soup. Put in 9 x 12 casserole dish. Top with potato puffs. Bake at 350° for 1 hour.

Sally Buck

CHEESY RICE, MUSHROOMS AND PEAS

1 (10 oz.) pkg. frozen peas,
  cooked and drained
1 (4.5 oz.) jar sliced
  mushrooms, drained
½ lb. Velveeta cheese, cubed
2 ½ c. cooked rice

Combine all in 1 ½-quart casserole and bake at 350° for 20 minutes. Makes 6 servings.

Barbara Fehr

CABBAGE ROLL CASSEROLE

1 lb. ground beef
½ c. onions
½ c. rice
½ tsp. salt
¼ tsp. pepper
1 can tomato soup
1 ½ c. water
¼ c. grated cheese
1 can chopped tomatoes

Chop cabbage. Spread in 9 x 13-inch pan. Brown onion and meat. Stir in rice, salt, pepper and tomatoes. Spoon over cabbage. Heat tomato soup and water to boiling. Pour over all. Sprinkle cheese. Cover with foil. Cook 1 ½ hours.

Patti Sitter

CHICKEN WITH RICE DINNER

1 c. uncooked Uncle Ben's rice
4 chicken breasts, halved

1 can cream of celery soup
1 can chicken broth

Spray a 9 x 13 pan with Pam. Put rice on bottom of pan and chicken on top of rice. Mix together the celery soup and chicken broth and pour over the chicken and rice. Cover pan with foil (airtight). Bake at 350° for 1 ½ hours.

Helen McKenzie

OVEN DINNER CASSEROLE

1 (16 oz.) pkg. frozen green beans
2 c. thinly sliced potatoes
1 tsp. salt
1 Tbsp. butter or margarine

1 can cream of mushroom soup
½ lb. ground beef, chicken or turkey

Place beans in greased 2-quart baking dish; top with potatoes. Dot with butter. Pour soup over vegetables. Cover and bake at 400° for 1 hour or until vegetables are tender, stirring once. Brown ground meat until almost done; drain. Place over vegetables. Bake, uncovered, 8 minutes longer. (Can be topped with cheese.)

Helen McKenzie

CROCK-POT CASSEROLE

4 potatoes, sliced
4 carrots, sliced
1 can peas and/or corn and/or green beans
1 onion, chopped

1 lb. lean hamburger, browned and drained
1 can tomato soup and 1 can of water, mixed

Add to crock-pot in order listed. Cook all day on low.

Cindy Andrus

PORK CHOP CASSEROLE

4 pork chops (1-inch thick)
1 can consomme
1 c. uncooked long grain rice
1 medium onion, chopped

½ c. Sauterne or other white
    table wine (can substitute
    white grape juice)
salt and pepper
pinch of thyme and
    marjoram

Use covered 2-quart casserole. Bake at 375° for 1 hour.
Brown chops slowly in large heavy skillet. Mix rice and
onion and spread in bottom of a 2-quart casserole. Place
chops on top. Mix consomme and wine (or juice); add water
to make 2 cups liquid. Add seasoning and heat to boiling.
Pour liquid over rice/onion mix and chops. Cover and bake
at 375° for 30 minutes. Remove cover and remove chops.
Stir rice and liquid mixture gently with a fork. Replace
chops and cover. Continue to bake for 30 minutes or until
chops are tender and rice absorbed all liquid. Turn chops
occasionally.

Martha Tomlinson

SEVEN LAYER CASSEROLE

Layer 1:

1 c. rice (Minute rice)

Layer 2:

1 c. whole kernel corn, drained

Layer 3:

½ c. chopped onion
¼ c. chopped bell pepper

½ tsp. salt
¼ tsp. pepper

Layer 4:

1 can tomato sauce

½ can water

Layer 5:

1 lb. hamburger meat
½ tsp. salt

¼ tsp. pepper

Layer 6:

1 can tomato sauce

¼ can water

MEATS & MAIN DISHES

Layer 7:

4 strips bacon

Lightly grease 2-quart casserole dish. Layer pan. Cover and bake in 375° oven for 30 minutes. Remove cover. Continue baking 15 to 20 minutes or until bacon is crisp. Cool 10 minutes.

❧ SPAGHETTI BAKE ❧

1 lb. ground beef
¾ c. finely chopped onion
½ c. finely chopped green pepper
1 can condensed cream of mushroom soup
1 can condensed tomato soup

1 soup can of water (1 ¼ c.)
1 (8 oz.) can tomato sauce
½ tsp. salt
1 clove garlic, minced
1 (8 oz.) pkg. spaghetti
1 c. shredded sharp process cheese

Combine beef, onion and green pepper in skillet. Stir and cook to lightly brown meat. Add soups, water, tomato sauce, salt and garlic. Heat.

Meanwhile, cook spaghetti by package directions; drain. blend ½ cup cheese and spaghetti into soup mixture. Turn into greased 3-quart casserole. Top with remaining ½ cup cheese. Bake at 350° about 45 minutes, until bubbling hot in center. Serves 8 to 10.

Karen Souder

❧ CHICKEN CASSEROLE ❧

1 box wild rice
4 to 5 lb. chicken, cooked and cut into pieces
2 cans chicken stock
2 cans mushroom soup

6 Tbsp. flour
6 Tbsp. butter
¾ lb. pkg. sharp cheese
1 large onion, chopped

Cook chicken. Cool. Chop. Mix together all ingredients except cheese. Sprinkle cheese over top. Use 9 x 13 pan. Bake until bubbly, 45 minutes.

TERIYAKI PORK TENDERLOIN
(Makes 8 servings.)

½ c. soy sauce
¼ c. olive or vegetable oil
4 tsp. brown sugar
2 tsp. ground ginger or less for double (3 tsp.)
1 tsp. pepper

2 garlic cloves, minced
4 pork tenderloins (¾ to 1 lb.)
coarsely ground pepper (optional)

Place in plastic bag. Seal. Turn to coat. Refrigerate 4 hours; turn. Grill.

Karen Souder

TUNA CHEESE IMPERIAL

1 (8 oz.) pkg. 1-inch wide noodles
½ c. margarine, divided into 5 Tbsp. and 3 Tbsp.
5 Tbsp. all-purpose flour
1 tsp. salt
¼ tsp. pepper
1 ½ c. milk
1 (8 oz.) pkg. cream cheese or low-fat cottage cheese
14 oz. tuna, drained and flaked

½ c. stuffed or ripe olives, sliced
2 Tbsp. chives, snipped
½ c. sliced mushrooms
½ to ¾ c. peas
1 carrot, diced (approximately)
1 c. broccoli florets, cut up
6 oz. Muenster cheese, sliced
1 ½ c. bread crumbs (rye or Italian bread preferred)

Cook noodles and drain. Melt 5 tablespoons margarine and stir in flour, salt and pepper. Stir until smooth and bubbly. Add milk and stir until it comes to the boil and thickens slightly. Turn down to a simmer and add cream cheese. Stir until melted. Add remaining ingredients except 3 tablespoons margarine, cheese and bread crumbs. Cook until heated through and well blended. Pour 1 cup of mixture into a 12-cup glass baking dish, then ½ of the noodles, ½ of the remaining sauce and ½ of the Muenster cheese. Repeat the layers. Melt 3 tablespoons margarine; add bread crumbs and stir until coated. Sprinkle over top of casserole and bake at 350°, uncovered, for 30 minutes. Serves 8 to 10.

Betty Ann Smith

TACO CASSEROLE

2 boxes Jiffy corn muffin
  mix
1 lb. ground beef
1 pkg. taco seasoning

1 can corn
1 c. chili beans
2 c. grated Cheddar cheese

Mix corn muffin mix according to package directions, adding corn to the mixture. Spoon ½ mixture into well-greased casserole dish. Brown ground beef. Add seasoning and chili beans. Spoon meat mixture over batter. Top beef with 1 cup cheese. Spoon remaining batter over that and add additional cheese. Bake at 350° about 30 minutes.

Janey Morell

REUBEN CASSEROLE

1 qt. sauerkraut, drained
8 oz. noodles, cooked and
  drained
1 (12 oz.) corned beef,
  shredded
½ c. onion, chopped
6 to 8 Swiss cheese slices

½ c. mayo
2 tsp. mustard
2 cans cream of mushroom
  soup
½ stick margarine
1 c. pumpernickel or
  seasoned bread crumbs

Layer sauerkraut and noodles in 9 x 12 pan. Layer onions and corned beef on noodles. Mix soup, mayo and mustard. Pour over casserole. Lay cheese slices on top and cover with bread crumbs. Slice pats of margarine over top. Bake at 350° for 45 minutes. Serves 6 to 8.

Kathy Lore

TURKEY POT PIE OR CHICKEN POT PIE

2 c. French green beans
2 c. potatoes, cubed
1 c. carrots, minced
2 ¼ c. turkey broth (can
  substitute chicken)
½ c. onion, chopped
¼ c. flour
2 Tbsp. margarine

1 Tbsp. parsley
½ tsp. marjoram leaves,
  crumbled
⅛ tsp. pepper
3 c. cubed turkey or chicken
¼ tsp. rosemary leaves,
  chopped
1 refrigerated pie crust

Combine beans, carrots and 1 cup broth. Bring to a boil. Cover and cook 10 minutes or until tender. Drain remaining broth. Add broth (2 cups). Saute in pan onions in 2 tablespoons butter or margarine until transparent. Stir in flour, parsley, marjoram, rosemary and pepper. Blend in the 2 cups broth. Bring to a boil, stirring frequently. Add vegetables and turkey. Turn into 2-quart shallow baking dish. Stretch pie crust over top. Cut several slits to vent. Bake at 400° for 35 minutes.

CRUNCHY CHICKEN BISCUIT CASSEROLE

2 c. cooked cubed chicken	4 oz. (1 c.) shredded cheese
10 ¾ oz. can condensed cream of chicken soup	½ c. mayonnaise
	1 tsp. lemon juice
8 ½ oz. can green beans, drained	10 oz. can refrigerated biscuits
2 ½ oz. jar sliced mushrooms (optional)	1 to 2 Tbsp. melted butter
	¼ to ½ c. cubed croutons

Heat oven to 375°. In medium saucepan, combine chicken, soup, beans, mushrooms, Cheddar, mayonnaise and lemon juice. Heat until hot and bubbly. Pour hot mixture into 2-quart baking dish. Separate biscuit dough into 10 biscuits. Arrange over mixture. Brush each biscuit with butter or margarine. Sprinkle with croutons. Bake at 375° for 25 to 30 minutes.

GARDEN VEGETABLE LASAGNA RECIPE

1 Tbsp. olive oil	¼ c. reserved liquid
½ c. diced onion	1 ½ tsp. dry basil leaves
3 tsp. minced garlic	1 ½ tsp. dry marjoram leaves
½ c. sliced mushrooms	pepper to taste
½ c. chopped yellow squash	1 c. fat-free Ricotta cheese
½ c. chopped zucchini	⅛ c. Parmesan cheese
½ c. eggplant, peeled and diced	¼ c. egg substitute
	1 Tbsp. chopped parsley
½ c. diced celery	1 ½ c. fat-free Mozzarella cheese, divided
½ c. diced carrot	
½ c. red pepper	6 pieces lasagna noodles, cooked according to pkg. directions and divided
½ c. green pepper	
28 oz. (1 can) whole peeled tomatoes in juice, quartered or crushed, drained and divided	

Preheat oven to 350°. In a heavy saucepan, heat oil and saute onion until translucent, about 3 minutes. Add garlic and saute for 2 minutes. Add mushrooms, yellow squash, zucchini, eggplant, celery, carrots and red and green peppers. Saute until tender. Add reserved tomato liquid and bring to a boil. Add basil, marjoram and 2 ¼ cups tomatoes. Season to taste with pepper; remove from heat and cool.

In a medium bowl, combine Ricotta cheese, Parmesan cheese, egg substitute and parsley. Set aside. Combine 1 ¼ cups Mozzarella cheese with the cooled vegetable mixture and set aside. In a 9 x 6-inch baking pan, layer 2 cooked noodles on the bottom. Cover with half of the Ricotta mixture and half of the vegetable mixture. Repeat using remaining mixture and noodles, ending with noodles on top. Cover with remaining 1 cup tomatoes and sprinkle with remaining ¼ cup Mozzarella cheese. Bake, covered, for 1 hour. Uncover and bake for an additional 30 minutes. Remove from oven. Let stand 15 minutes before serving.

Michelle Wobrak

–•EXTRA RECIPES•–

Recipe

Page Number

MEATS & MAIN DISHES

Vegetables

Recipe Favorites

Page No.

Recipe Title:_____

_____ _____

_____ _____

_____ _____

_____ _____

_____ _____

_____ _____

_____ _____

_____ _____

Family Favorites

Page No.

Recipe Title:_____

_____ _____

_____ _____

_____ _____

_____ _____

Notes:_____

_____

_____

_____

VEGETABLES

 ## GREEN BEAN CASSEROLE
(Serves 6; Preparation Time: 45 Minutes.)

1 (10.75 oz.) can cream of
   mushroom soup
¾ c. milk
1 ⅓ c. French's® French
   fried onions

2 (14.5 oz.) cans Del Monte®
   green beans, drained
4 slices bacon, cooked and
   crumbled

Cook bacon and crumble. Preheat oven to 350°. In a
1 ½-quart baking dish, combine soup, milk, ⅔ cup of French
fried onions, green beans and bacon. Bake for 30 minutes or
until hot. Stir. Top with remaining onions. Bake an additional 5 minutes.

BAKED CORN

2 eggs
½ c. milk
2 tsp. butter

2 tsp. flour
2 tsp. sugar
1 can corn

Bake at 350° for 45 minutes.

Delores Demichele

BUTTERNUT SQUASH BAKE

⅓ c. margarine
¾ c. sugar
2 eggs
1 (5 oz.) can evaporated milk

1 tsp. vanilla
2 c. mashed butternut
   squash

Topping:

½ c. crisp rice cereal
¼ c. packed brown sugar

¼ c. chopped nuts
2 Tbsp. margarine

Cream butter and sugar. Beat in eggs, milk and vanilla. Stir in squash (mixture will be thin). Pour into greased 11 x 7 x 2-inch baking pan. Bake, uncovered, at 350° for 45 minutes or until almost set.

Combine topping ingredients. Sprinkle over casserole. Return to oven for 5 to 10 minutes.

Sally Buck

❧ BAKED PINTO BEANS ❧

2 c. beans
3 Tbsp. sorghum (molasses)
1 medium onion, sliced
3 Tbsp. catsup

1 tsp. mustard
4 strips bacon, fried and
  crumbled

Repeat for additional layers. Bake at 350°. Watch that it doesn't dry out.

Jackie Wallace

❧ POTATOES PICASSO ❧

1 (32 oz.) pkg. frozen hash
  brown potatoes
4 c. (16 oz.) shredded sharp
  natural Cheddar cheese
1 can cream of chicken soup

1 pt. dairy sour cream
1 c. chopped onion
½ c. margarine, melted
crushed corn flakes

Combine potatoes, cheese, soup, sour cream, onion and ¼ cup margarine. Mix well. Place in 13 ½ x 8 ¾-inch greased baking dish. Combine corn flakes and remaining margarine. Sprinkle over potato mixture. Bake at 350° for 1 hour and 15 minutes.

Patti Sitter

❧ SCALLOPED CORN ❧

1 can creamed corn
1 can whole kernel corn
2 eggs

8 oz. sour cream
1 stick melted margarine
1 box Jiffy corn bread mix

Mix all together and bake at 350° for 45 minutes.

Rita Donner

❧ BEST BAKED BEANS ❧

1 can pork and beans	⅛ c. molasses
3 Tbsp. mustard	⅛ c. brown sugar

Add chopped onion and bacon bits. Drain can of beans. Pour into a casserole dish, adding all ingredients. Bake at 350° for 60 to 75 minutes.

Rita Donner

❧ CARROT PENNIES ❧

½ c. tomato soup	1 c. diced peppers (if
½ c. chopped onions	desired)

Sauce:

½ c. vinegar	⅛ c. oil
1 c. sugar	½ tsp. prepared mustard

Put cooked carrots in casserole. Bring sauce to boil. Pour hot sauce over carrots. Will keep 1 month in refrigerator.

Rita Donner

❧ BAKED CORN ❧

1 can creamed corn	2 Tbsp. cornstarch
1 can evaporated milk	2 eggs
1 Tbsp. sugar	

Blend together. Pour into buttered baking dish. Bake until brown, about 1 hour.

Dorothy Lytle

❧ BRANDIED SWEET POTATOES ❧

8 medium sweet potatoes	½ c. golden raisins
1 ¼ c. brown sugar, packed	½ c. chopped walnuts
½ c. water	½ c. brandy
¼ c. butter or margarine	

Wash potatoes but do not peel. Boil in water to cover until barely tender, about 15 minutes. Cool, peel and slice ¼-inch thick. Arrange potato slices in overlapping layers in buttered 13 x 9-inch casserole. Bring brown sugar, water, butter and raisins to boil in saucepan; turn off heat. Add walnuts and brandy; pour over potatoes. Bake, uncovered, in a preheated 350° oven 30 minutes, basting several times with syrup in the casserole.

Agnes Billisits

❧ BAKED BEANS ❧

1 lb. can butter beans	1 tsp. baking soda
3 lb. can navy beans	½ pkg. Lipton onion soup
7 oz. ketchup	mix
1 c. brown sugar	1 Tbsp. mustard (jar type)

Pour syrups into mixture; cover with raw bacon strips. Bake at 350° for 1 hour.

Agnes Billisits

❧ ZUCCHINI PANCAKES ❧

1 ½ c. grated unpeeled zucchini, pressed dry between paper towels	¼ c. flour
	2 eggs
	2 Tbsp. mayonnaise
2 Tbsp. grated or finely chopped onion	¼ tsp. oregano
	salt and pepper to taste
¼ c. Parmesan cheese	

Mix together. Melt 1 tablespoon butter in 8 ½ or 10-inch Rangetoppers skillet. Spoon batter (2 heaping tablespoons makes a nice size) into skillet. Flatten with spatula. Cook over medium heat until browned on both sides. Serve plain or top with tomato sauce and grated cheese or sour cream and chives. (Makes a terrific accompaniment for chicken, roasts or chops.) Serves 2 to 3.

Agnes Billisits

❧ CARROT CASSEROLE ❧

2 lb. carrots, sliced, cooked and drained	1 tsp. salt
	⅛ tsp. pepper
¼ c. margarine	½ tsp. prepared mustard
½ c. onion, chopped	½ c. Cheddar cheese,
¼ c. flour	shredded
2 c. milk	

Saute onion in margarine and add next 5 ingredients to make white sauce. In a 2-quart greased casserole, layer half of the carrots, white sauce and the cheese. Layer the rest of the carrots and pour remaining sauce over all. Top with buttered bread crumbs. Bake at 350° for 25 minutes.

Nancy Root

🌿 CABBAGE CASSEROLE 🌿
(Delicious!)

2 lb. cabbage	1 (15 oz.) can tomato sauce
2 lb. lean ground beef	2 tsp. salt
¾ lb. Swiss cheese, grated	⅛ tsp. pepper
2 cans tomato soup	⅛ tsp. garlic powder

Heat oven to 350°. Coarsely chop cabbage. Combine soup, sauce and seasonings. Use Dutch oven and spray with Pam. Cover pan bottom with sauce, thin layer. Layer as follows: ¼ of cabbage, ⅓ of ground beef (raw and crumbled), ⅓ of Swiss cheese and ¼ of sauce (tomato). Repeat for total of 3 layers. Top with remaining ¼ cabbage and sauce. Bake 2 hours. Serves 4 to 6. FREEZES WELL.

🌿 ZUCCHINI BAKE 🌿

6 c. diced zucchini	2 Tbsp. tomato paste
1 lb. cubed or chunked	1 large can stewed tomatoes
pepperoni	½ c. shredded or grated
1 tsp. oregano	Parmesan cheese

Combine ingredients in casserole dish. Top with seasoned bread crumbs. Bake for 350° for an hour.

Judy Nass

🌿 CALICO BEANS 🌿

½ lb. bacon	1 (21 oz.) can pork and beans
1 lb. hamburg	(do not drain)
1 (15 oz.) can kidney beans	1 Tbsp. dry mustard
(do not drain)	2 Tbsp. vinegar
1 (15 oz.) can butter beans	1 c. ketchup
(do not drain)	½ c. brown sugar
	1 chopped onion

Cut up bacon. Fry crisp. Brown beef and onion; drain. Add to other ingredients in large casserole at 400° for 1 hour or crock-pot.

Delores Demichele

CALICO BEANS

1 lb. hamburg
½ lb. bacon
½ c. ketchup
1 tsp. salt
¾ c. brown sugar
1 tsp. mustard

2 tsp. vinegar
1 (No. 2) can pork and beans
1 (No. 2) can kidney beans
1 (No. 2) can lima beans,
    drain lima beans only

Brown hamburg and bacon. Cut bacon into pieces. Put into casserole and add all other ingredients. Mix well. Bake at 350° for 40 minutes. Makes 6 to 8 servings.

Phyllis Pierce

3-CHEESE BROCCOLI BAKE

1 c. Bisquick
¼ c. milk
2 eggs
½ c. grated Parmesan cheese
1 (12 oz.) carton cottage
    cheese

1 (10 oz.) pkg. frozen
    chopped broccoli, thawed
4 oz. Monterey Jack cheese,
    cut in cubes
2 eggs

Heat oven to 375°. Grease rectangular baking dish. Mix Bisquick, milk and 2 eggs; beat vigorously 20 strokes. Spread in baking dish. Mix remaining ingredients. Spoon evenly over batter in dish. Bake until set, about 30 minutes.

Helen McKenzie

ZUCCHINI LASAGNE

½ lb. ground beef
1 (15 oz.) can tomato sauce
½ tsp. salt
⅛ tsp. pepper
1 c. cottage cheese
1 medium onion
1 tsp. oregano

½ tsp. basil
1 egg
2 Tbsp. flour
1 c. shredded Mozzarella
    cheese
4 medium zucchini

Cook ground beef and onion. Drain. Add tomato sauce, salt, oregano, basil and pepper. Simmer about 5 minutes. Slice unpeeled zucchini lengthwise into ¼-inch slices. Combine egg and cottage cheese. In bottom of 8 x 12 baking dish, arrange half of zucchini and sprinkle with a tablespoon of flour. Top with cottage cheese mixture and half of meat mixture. Repeat with remaining zucchini and flour; sprinkle with Mozzarella cheese and remaining meat mixture. Bake 1 hour at 325° or until zucchini is fork-tender. Let stand 10 minutes before serving.

Audrey Evans

 VEGETABLE RISOTTO

2 Tbsp. olive oil, divided
1 medium zucchini, cubed
1 medium yellow summer
  squash, cubed
1 c. shiitake mushroom
  slices
1 c. chopped onions
1 clove garlic, minced

6 plum tomatoes, quartered
  and seeded
1 tsp. dried oregano leaves
3 c. vegetable stock
¾ c. Arborio rice
¼ c. grated Parmesan cheese
salt
black pepper
½ c. frozen peas, thawed

Heat 1 tablespoon oil in large saucepan over medium heat until hot. Add zucchini and summer squash; cook and stir 5 minutes or until crisp-tender. Place in medium bowl; set aside. Add mushrooms, onions and garlic to saucepan. Cook and stir 5 minutes or until tender. Add tomatoes and oregano; cook and stir 2 to 3 minutes or until tomatoes are soft. Place in bowl with zucchini mixture. Wipe saucepan clean with paper towels. Place stock in small saucepan. Bring to a boil over medium heat. Reduce heat to medium-low to keep stock hot, but not boiling. Heat remaining 1 tablespoon oil in saucepan over medium heat until hot. Add rice. Cook and stir 2 minutes. Using ladle or measuring cup, add ¾ cup stock to rice. Reduce heat to medium-low maintaining a simmer. Cook and stir until rice has absorbed stock. Repeat, adding stock 3 more times, cooking and stirring until rice has absorbed stock. (Total cooking time of rice is about 20 to 25 minutes.) Stir cheese into rice mixture. Season to taste with salt and pepper. Stir in reserved vegetables and peas. Cook until heated through. Serve immediately. Garnish, if desired.

Michelle Wobrak

ASPARAGUS IN VINAIGRETTE
(Easter time great dish.)

2 lb. fresh asparagus,
    trimmed and cut into
    2-inch pieces
2 green onions, chopped
2 Tbsp. diced green pepper
2 Tbsp. sweet pickle relish
1 garlic clove, minced

⅓ c. olive oil
2 Tbsp. lemon juice
1 Tbsp. diced onion
1 Tbsp. minced fresh parsley
¾ tsp. salt
¼ tsp. pepper

Place asparagus in a steamer basket. Place in a sauce-pan over 1-inch of water; bring to a boil. Cover and steam for 6 to 8 minutes or until crisp-tender. Rinse with cold water; drain well. Place in a large bowl; add the green onions, green pepper, pickle relish and garlic. In a small bowl, whisk the oil, lemon juice, onion, parsley, salt and pepper. Pour over asparagus mixture and toss to coat. Cover and refrigerate until chilled. Serve with a slotted spoon. Yield: 8 servings.

Louise Johnson

FANCY BAKED BEANS

½ lb. bacon
1 small onion
2 (16 oz.) cans pork and
    beans
2 (16 oz.) cans kidney beans

2 (16 oz.) cans butter beans
1 c. brown sugar
1 c. ketchup
4 Tbsp. Worcestershire sauce
½ lb. grated Cheddar cheese

Chop bacon and onion; brown and drain fat. Drain beans well and combine. Combine remaining ingredients and mix in bowl. Combine all ingredients in casserole dish. Bake, covered, at 350° for 1 hour.

Carol Eckert

TOPPING FOR CORN-ON-THE-COB

½ c. mayonnaise (not light or
    Miracle Whip)
⅛ c. Parmesan cheese

lime juice (use enough to
    make creamy mixture)
cayenne pepper to taste

Blend all ingredients together. Proportions can be changed to suit tastes. Fresh limes are better. Spread evenly over hot corn instead of butter.

❧ SWEET POTATO CASSEROLE ❧

3 c. sweet potatoes or yams,
  well drained
½ c. butter
2 eggs

1 tsp. vanilla
½ c. sugar
¼ tsp. cinnamon

Beat with electric mixer and put in shallow baking dish.

Topping:

1 c. brown sugar
⅓ c. flour

½ c. butter
1 c. chopped walnuts

Soften butter and mix all ingredients. Sprinkle over potato mixture. Bake, uncovered, at 350° for 30 minutes.

❧ POTATO CASSEROLE ❧

1 box/bag (1 lb. 8 oz.) hash
  brown potato squares,
  thawed and cubed
1 can cream of chicken soup
1 (8 oz.) pkg. shredded
  Cheddar (low-fat)
½ c. chopped onions

1 pt. low-fat or no-fat sour
  cream
1 tsp. salt
¼ c. butter, melted and
  mixed with crushed
  cornflakes

Preheat oven to 350°. Mix all ingredients except buttered cornflake crumbs and potatoes. Fold in potatoes. Turn into greased casserole dish. Top with buttered cornflake crumbs. Bake at 350° for an hour. Recipe can be doubled, but will need to bake longer. Can be prepared ahead.

Michelle Wobrak

❧ CABBAGE AND POTATO BAKE ❧

1 cabbage (about 2 to 2 ½ lb.)
2 large Idaho potatoes
  (about 2 ½ lb.)
12 oz. lean bacon, sliced
  into ½-inch pieces

2 c. yellow onions, peeled
  and sliced lengthwise
1 tsp. salt
1 tsp. ground black pepper
2 c. low sodium fat-free
  chicken broth

Preheat oven to 350°. Rinse cabbage in cold water, removing tough outer leaves. Cut the cabbage into quarters and remove the hard core. Cut the cabbage quarters into halves and place, rounded side down, in a roasting pan. Peel the potatoes. Cut in half crosswise, then the halves into quarters. Arrange potatoes in the roasting pan. Fry the bacon for 7 minutes. Add the sliced onions, salt and black pepper to the pan with the bacon and cook until soft, about 5 minutes. Evenly distribute the bacon mixture and pan drippings over the potatoes and cabbage in the roasting pan. Pour the chicken broth over the whole mixture. Tightly cover the pan with aluminum foil. Bake for 1 ½ hours. Remove the pan from the oven and allow to sit, covered, for 15 minutes before serving. Serve the cabbage and potatoes with the bacon and broth spooned over them.

Michelle Wobrak

🌿 CREAMY MACARONI AND 🌿 CHEESE

2 c. elbow macaroni
¼ c. butter
6 Tbsp. flour
1 tsp. salt

2 c. milk
2 c. grated sharp Cheddar
   cheese

Cook macaroni in 3 cups water in microwave for 10 minutes. Drain and put back in casserole dish. On stove top, melt butter. Blend in salt. Stir in milk until smooth. Stir every minute until thickened. Stir in cheese until melted. Stir sauce into macaroni, mixing well. Microwave on High 7 to 10 minutes, stirring every 4 minutes. If desired, sprinkle top with bread crumbs (buttered) or paprika.

🌿 SCALLOPED POTATOES 🌿

3 Tbsp. butter
2 Tbsp. flour
1 tsp. salt
¼ tsp. pepper

2 c. milk
3 ½ to 4 c. thinly sliced
   potatoes
2 Tbsp. minced onions

Place butter in 1-quart measuring cup. Microwave on High 30 seconds. Blend in flour, salt and pepper. Gradually stir in milk. Microwave 8 to 10 minutes, stirring after every

4 minutes. Add potatoes and onions, in layers; do half potatoes, onion and sauce in greased 2-quart casserole. Repeat layers. Cover and microwave 17 to 19 minutes. Remove and let stand 5 minutes before serving.

❧ VEGETABLE CASSEROLE ❧

1 bag mixed vegetables
  (broccoli, carrot,
  cauliflower)
1 can cream of mushroom
  soup

1 c. Swiss cheese
⅓ c. sour cream
pepper to taste
1 can French fried onions

Combine first 5 ingredients. Top with onions. Bake in 350° oven for 30 minutes.

❧ BROCCOLI CASSEROLE ❧

2 (10 oz.) pkg. frozen
  broccoli, cooked as
  directed

1 small pkg. stuffing mix,
  cooked as directed
1 can cream of mushroom
  soup

Place in dish in layers. Bake at 350° for 1 hour.
Cooked chicken breast or turkey, cut up, can also be added, if desired.

Kathy Lore

❧ CHEESE BROCCOLI AND RICE ❧ CASSEROLE

1 (8 oz.) jar Cheez Whiz
1 (20 oz.) frozen chopped
  broccoli
2 pkg. Boil-in-Bag rice = 1 c.

1 can creamed mushroom
  soup (rinse can out with
  milk)
1 stick oleo

Mix all together. Microwave or bake about 20 minutes. Stir up so well mixed.

Delores Demichele

❧ RICE-BROCCOLI STUFF ❧

1 c. Minute rice (not cooked)
1 c. water
½ c. chopped onion
1 can mushroom soup
1 (10 oz.) pkg. chopped
  frozen broccoli

½ c. Cheddar cheese (to be
  added last)
½ c. chopped celery
½ c. melted butter

Put all in casserole, except cheese. Bake at 350° for 45 minutes. Take out. Top with cheese. Bake for 15 more minutes.

Karen Souder

❧ CHEESY HASH BROWN BAKE ❧

1 (32 oz.) pkg. Southern style
  frozen hash brown
  potatoes, thawed
2 c. (8 oz.) shredded Cheddar
  cheese

1 c. (11 oz.) condensed
  Cheddar cheese soup
1 c. sour cream
¾ c. sliced green onion

Preheat oven to 375°. In large bowl, combine all ingredients. Spread mixture into greased 9 x 13 pan. Bake 50 to 60 minutes or until lightly browned and bubbly.

❧ BROCCOLI, CHEESE, RICE CASSEROLE ❧

1 (8 oz.) jar Cheez Whiz (big
  jar will do)
1 (20 oz.) frozen chopped
  broccoli

2 pkg. Boil-in-Bag rice
1 can cream mushroom soup
  (rinse can out with milk)
1 stick oleo

Mix all together. Put in oven for about 20 minutes or more. Mix up good.

Delores Demichele

❧ PINEAPPLE CASSEROLE ❧

2 (16 oz.) pineapple tidbits,
  drained
2 c. mild Cheddar cheese,
  grated

1 stick margarine
½ c. sugar
3 Tbsp. flour
1 stack Ritz crackers

Place pineapple into greased baking dish, after tossing thoroughly with sugar, flour and grated cheese. Melt margarine. Add crushed crackers to coat. Spread on pineapple mixture. Bake at 350° for 30 minutes.

Audrey Evans

❧ VEGETABLE CASSEROLE ❧

¾ c. milk
1 can cream of mushroom
soup
2 (16 oz.) pkg. frozen
broccoli, cauliflower and
carrots mix

1 ⅓ c. French fried onions,
divided
grated Parmesan cheese

In 1 ½-quart casserole, mix together all ingredients except I divided (⅔ cup) French fried onions and cheese. Sprinkle top with remaining French fried onions and cheese. Bake 30 to 35 minutes at 350°.

Martha Tomlinson

❧ VEGETABLE CASSEROLE ❧

1 c. diced cooked carrots
1 c. diced cooked peas
1 c. diced cooked green
beans
1 c. cooked kernel corn
¼ tsp. salt
pinch of pepper
4 Tbsp. butter
1 c. chopped medium onion
½ c. chopped celery

2 Tbsp. red or green pepper
4 Tbsp. flour
2 c. milk
½ tsp. salt
dash of cayenne pepper
½ c. shredded Cheddar
cheese
¼ c. dried bread crumbs
1 Tbsp. butter

Combine carrots, peas, beans and corn in a bowl. Add salt and pepper. Toss lightly with fork. Melt butter in skillet. Add onion, celery and red pepper and cook over low heat until onion is tender, not brown. Sprinkle in flour and blend. Gradually add milk and cook, stirring constantly, until thickened. Add salt, cayenne pepper and cheese. Stir until cheese is melted. Arrange alternate layers of vegetables and cheese sauce in greased 2-quart casserole, ending with cheese sauce on top. Sprinkle with bread crumbs and dot with butter. Refrigerate until needed. Bake, uncovered, at 350° for 45 minutes. Serves 8.

Especially good for Christmas or other times of celebration. So colorful and yummy!

Gloria Love

YOUR FAVORITE RECIPES

Recipe   **Page Number**

Breads, Rolls and Pastries

Recipe Favorites

Page No. _____

Recipe Title:_____

_____ _____

_____ _____

_____ _____

_____ _____

_____ _____

_____ _____

_____ _____

_____ _____

_____ _____

_____ _____

Family Favorites

Page No. _____

Recipe Title:_____

_____ _____

_____ _____

_____ _____

_____ _____

_____ _____

Notes:_____

_____

_____

BREADS, ROLLS & PASTRIES

❧ PUMPKIN MUFFINS ❧

2 eggs
1 c. milk
1 stick butter
1 c. granulated sugar
2 c. flour
1 ¼ c. canned pumpkin

2 tsp. baking powder
1 tsp. cinnamon
¼ tsp. nutmeg
¼ tsp. salt
½ c. nuts
½ c. raisins

Cream butter, sugar and pumpkin until smooth. Add eggs. Blend all 4 ingredients well. Sift flour, baking powder and spices and add alternately with milk to egg mixture. Do not overmix. Fold in nuts and raisins. Sprinkle little cinnamon and sugar on top before baking. Bake in greased muffin tins at 375° for 25 minutes or until done. Serves 2 dozen.

Karen Souder

❧ ZUCCHINI PIE ❧

4 c. zucchini
1 ¼ c. sugar
1 tsp. cinnamon

1 tsp. cream of tartar
3 Tbsp. flour

Pare, seed and slice zucchini. Slice lengthwise 2 times, then seed and slice. Boil with lemon juice and water (splash) until soft; drain, then mix with other ingredients. Empty into unbaked pie shell. Bake at 400° for 40 minutes.

Crumb Topping:

1 c. flour
½ c. firm butter

½ c. brown sugar

Use crumb topping or pie crust top.

Kathy Lore

🌿 SIX-WEEKS MUFFINS 🌿

5 c. flour
3 c. sugar
1 c. melted shortening (cool)
1 tsp. salt

5 tsp. soda
1 (15 oz.) pkg. Raisin Bran
4 beaten eggs
1 qt. buttermilk

Store in refrigerator; use as needed. Bake approximately 20 minutes at 350° in cupcake tins. Makes about 4 dozen.

Agnes Billisits

🌿 COCONUT CREAM PIE 🌿

⅓ c. sugar
2 Tbsp. + 2 tsp. cornstarch
¼ tsp. salt
3 egg yolks

2 c. scalded milk (double boiler)
1 Tbsp. butter
1 tsp. vanilla
High Never Fail Meringue

Add sugar, cornstarch and salt to egg yolks. Pour scalded milk into sugar mixture gradually and blend. Return to double boiler. Stir and cook until thickened. Add butter and vanilla. Pour into baked 7 ½ or 8-inch crust. Cover with High Never Fail Meringue. Sprinkle with coconut. Brown in 350° oven.

High Never Fail Meringue:

1 Tbsp. cornstarch
2 Tbsp. cold water
pinch of salt
½ c. water

3 egg whites
⅛ tsp. cream of tartar
6 Tbsp. sugar
½ tsp. vanilla

Cook over low heat the cornstarch, 2 tablespoons cold water and salt. Blend cornstarch, water and salt to make paste. Add ½ cup water. Cook, stirring constantly, until clear. Cool, but don't chill. Beat egg whites, cream of tartar and sugar until peaks form. Add custard to egg whites with vanilla. Beat together and spread on pie. Brown. "Looks like a bakery pie."

Helen Irvin

🌿 BANANA BREAD 🌿

1 c. sugar	2 ½ c. flour
2 eggs	1 tsp. baking powder
½ c. shortening	1 tsp. baking soda
4 medium mashed bananas	½ c. chopped nuts
8 Tbsp. buttermilk	½ tsp. salt

Grease and flour loaf pans. Bake at 350° until done.

Dorothy Lytle

🌿 PUMPKIN BREAD 🌿

3 ½ c. flour	1 tsp. salt
3 c. sugar	4 eggs
1 tsp. baking powder	¾ c. water
1 tsp. baking soda	1 c. oil
1 tsp. cinnamon	2 c. pumpkin
1 tsp. nutmeg	1 c. chopped nuts

Mix together. Bake at 350° about 1 hour. Grease loaf pans.

Dorothy Lytle

🌿 STRAWBERRY NUT BREAD 🌿

2 pkg. (10 oz.) frozen strawberries	2 c. sugar
	3 tsp. cinnamon
4 eggs	1 tsp. baking soda
1 ¼ c. salad oil	1 tsp. salt
3 c. flour	1 c. nuts

Combine thawed strawberries, eggs and oil. In large bowl, combine flour, sugar, cinnamon, baking soda, salt and nuts. Add strawberry mixture to dry ingredients. Stir until blended. Bake 1 hour. Makes 2 loaf pans.

Patty Webber

🌿 PUMPKIN BREAD 🌿

3 ½ c. flour	1 tsp. salt
3 c. sugar	4 eggs
1 tsp. baking powder	¾ c. water
1 tsp. baking soda	1 c. oil
1 tsp. cinnamon	2 c. pumpkin
1 tsp. nutmeg	1 c. chopped nuts

Mix together. Bake at 350° about 1 hour. Grease loaf pans.

Dorothy Lytle

BUTTERSCOTCH PIE

2 c. milk
6 Tbsp. flour
1 ½ c. brown sugar
⅛ tsp. salt

2 egg yolks, beaten
3 Tbsp. butter
1 tsp. vanilla
meringue

Scald milk; add flour and sugar. Stir to a smooth paste in a little cold milk. Cook 15 minutes in double boiler. Add a little hot mixture to yolks. Return to double boiler and cook 2 to 3 minutes. Add butter and flavoring. Pour into baked crust. Cover with meringue. Bake 20 minutes.

I use light brown sugar.

Jean Lydic

CHOCOLATE LOVERS SILK PIE

2 pkg. (4 oz.) Baker's
German's sweet chocolate
1 (8 oz.) pkg. cream cheese
3 ½ c. Cool Whip

½ c. milk (used in two ¼ c.
portions)
2 Tbsp. sugar
1 chocolate wafer crumb
crust (Oreo)

Heat all but 3 squares of chocolate with ¼ cup of milk in large mixing bowl on High for about 1 ½ to 2 minutes. Stir after microwaving until chocolate and milk are blended. Gently stir in Cool Whip until smooth. Spoon into crust and freeze until firm. Let stand about 30 minutes before serving. Before serving, melt the rest of the chocolate and drizzle over pie.

SWEDISH APPLE PIE

Step 1:

1 tsp. cinnamon
1 tsp. sugar

2 ½ c. sliced apples

Step 2:

1 c. sugar
1 ¼ sticks margarine, melted

1 c. flour
1 egg, beaten

Grease a 9-inch pie plate with butter. Fill ⅔ full with apples. Sprinkle with cinnamon and sugar.

In a separate bowl, mix sugar and butter, adding flour and egg; mix well. Pour and spread over apples. Bake at 350° for 65 minutes.

Kathy Lore

❧ SCHITZ 'UN KNEPP ❧
(Pa. Dutch Dish)

ham	4 tsp. baking powder
2 Tbsp. brown sugar	¼ tsp. pepper
dried sweet apples	1 beaten egg
2 c. flour	milk
1 tsp. salt	3 Tbsp. melted butter

Cook ham with brown sugar. Wash apples. Cover with hot water and soak overnight. Add the apples and the water in which they were soaking to the ham and cook for an hour.

Make dumplings by sifting flour, salt, baking powder and pepper. Stir in egg and milk to stiffen dough but should be moist; add butter. Remove apples and ham from liquid. Drop dough by spoonfuls into the HOT ROLLING BOIL. Cover kettle tight and cook dumplings for 15 minutes. Do not remove lid from kettle while cooking dumplings.

Karen Souder

❧ EASY PECAN PIE ❧

2 beaten eggs	2 Tbsp. melted butter
1 c. corn syrup	1 Tbsp. sugar
1 tsp. vanilla	⅓ tsp. salt

Pour into unbaked crust and sprinkle with ½ cup chopped pecans. (I use pecan halves.) Bake at 450° for 10 minutes and then 325° for 30 minutes.

Jackie Wallace

❧ AMAZING COCONUT PIE ❧
(Biscuit mix makes crust, only clean up blender.)

2 c. milk	½ c. butter or oleo
¾ c. sugar	1 ½ tsp. vanilla
½ c. biscuit mix	1 c. flake coconut
4 eggs	

Combine all except coconut in blender. Cover and blend on low speed 3 minutes. Pour into 9-inch greased pie pan; let stand 5 minutes, then sprinkle with coconut. Bake at 350° for 40 minutes. Serve warm or cool.

                                                        Barbara Fehr

🌿 LEMON PIE 🌿

4 egg yolks (save whites for   6 Tbsp. cornstarch
  meringue)   salt
½ c. lemon juice   2 ¼ c. boiling water
1 ½ c. sugar

Stir together egg yolks and lemon juice. In saucepan, mix together sugar, cornstarch and salt. Add water. Cook until thick. Add egg and lemon juice, stirring constantly. Cook until blended. Pour into baked crust. Top with meringue, making sure it touches the crust. Brown in oven. Cool and serve.

                                                        Jackie Wallace

🌿 PENNSYLVANIA DUTCH PIE 🌿 CRUST

3 c. flour   1 egg, well beaten
1 tsp. salt   5 Tbsp. water
1 ½ c. shortening   1 tsp. vinegar

Blend flour, salt and shortening. Add egg, water and vinegar. Makes just 2 double crust pies.

                                                        Myrna Brown
                                                        Eric, PA

🌿 SAVORY PARTY BREAD 🌿

1 unsliced round loaf (1 lb.)   ½ c. butter or margarine,
  sourdough bread   melted
1 lb. Monterey Jack cheese,   ½ c. chopped green onions
  sliced   2 to 3 tsp. poppy seeds

Cut the bread lengthwise and crosswise without cutting through the bottom crust. Insert cheese between cuts. Combine butter, onions and poppy seeds; drizzle over the bread. Wrap in foil; place on a baking sheet. Bake at 350° for 15 minutes. Unwrap; bake 10 minutes longer or until the cheese is melted. Yield: 6 to 8 servings.

Leigh Ann Gigliotti

🌿 ORANGE-GLAZED CRULLERS 🌿

1 (¼ oz.) pkg. active dry
  yeast
¼ c. warm water (110° to
  115°)
¾ c. warm milk (110° to 115°)
½ c. butter or margarine,
  softened

¼ c. sugar
1 tsp. salt
2 eggs, beaten
4 c. all-purpose flour
oil (for deep-fat frying)

Glaze:

2 c. confectioners sugar
3 Tbsp. orange juice

1 tsp. grated orange peel

In a mixing bowl, dissolve yeast in water. Add milk, butter, sugar, salt and eggs; mix well. Beat in 2 cups flour until smooth. Add remaining flour. Place in a greased bowl, turning once to grease top. Cover and refrigerate overnight.

Punch dough down; divide in half. Return one portion to the refrigerator. On a floured surface, roll out second portion into an 18 x 9-inch rectangle; cut widthwise into ¾-inch strips. Fold each strip in half lengthwise and twist several times. Pinch ends to seal. Place on greased baking sheets. Repeat with the remaining dough. Cover and let rise until almost doubled, about 35 to 45 minutes. In an electric skillet or deep-fat fryer, heat oil to 375°. Fry crullers, a few at a time, until golden, about 1 minute on each side, turning with a slotted spoon. Drain on paper towels. Combine glaze ingredients; brush over warm crullers. Yield: about 3 dozen.

Leigh Ann Gigliotti

🌿 HOBBIT BREAD 🌿

butter (to grease loaf pans)
graham cracker or bread
  crumbs
3 eggs, yolks and whites
  separated
pinch of sugar
pinch of salt
⅓ c. sugar
1 ¾ c. flour

¾ tsp. baking powder
⅓ tsp. baking soda
⅔ c. sour cream
6 Tbsp. poppy seeds
⅓ c. orange juice
grated rind of 1 orange
1 tsp. vanilla
1 stick butter
¾ c. sugar

Preheat oven to 325°. Grease loaf pans with the butter and coat with crumbs. Set aside. Separate the eggs; reserve the yolks. Place the whites in a small mixing bowl. Add the pinch of sugar and salt to whites. Start beating the egg whites on low speed. Continue beating on low speed until the whites start to thicken and turn opaque. Turn the mixer to high speed, gradually adding ⅓ cup sugar. The egg whites are often ready at this point. If not, continue beating on high speed until the egg whites form stiff peaks, but are not dry. Set aside.

In small mixing bowl, combine the wet mix consisting of sour cream, poppy seeds, orange juice, orange rind and vanilla. Set aside. In large mixing bowl, cream together the butter and ¾ cup sugar. Slowly add 3 egg yolks. On mixer's low speed, alternately add the dry and wet mix, beginning and ending with the dry mix. Take a small amount of the egg whites and stir into the batter to loosen. Then lightly, but thoroughly, fold the remaining egg whites into the batter. Pour equally into 2 loaf pans which should be baked at 325° for 1 to 1¼ hours. When a toothpick inserted into the middle is dry, the bread is done. Allow to cool 3 to 5 minutes before turning out onto the rack.

Betty Ann Smith

❧ MONKEY BREAD ❧

½ c. granulated sugar
3 tsp. cinnamon
½ c. (1 stick) butter
1 c. packed brown sugar
1 (8 oz.) pkg. cream cheese

2 (12 oz.) cans refrigerated
   biscuits (10 count)
1 ½ c. coarsely chopped
   walnuts

Preheat the oven to 350°. Spray a Bundt pan with nonstick cooking spray. Mix the granulated sugar and cinnamon. In a saucepan, melt the butter and brown sugar over low heat, stirring well; set aside. Cut the cream cheese into 20 equal cubes. Press the biscuits out with your fingers and sprinkle each with ½ teaspoon of cinnamon sugar. Place a cube of cream cheese in the center of each biscuit, wrapping and sealing the dough around the cream cheese. Sprinkle ½ cup of the nuts into the bottom of the Bundt pan. Place half of the prepared biscuits in the pan. Sprinkle with cinnamon sugar; pour half of the melted butter mixture over the biscuits and sprinkle on ½ cup of nuts. Layer the remaining biscuits on top; sprinkle with the remaining cinnamon sugar. Pour the remaining butter mixture over the biscuits and sprinkle with the remaining ½ cup of nuts. Bake for 30 minutes. Remove from the oven and cool for 5 minutes. Place a plate on top and invert.

Betty Ann Smith

❧ BANANA BREAD ❧

2 eggs
½ c. soft margarine
1 c. sugar
1 ½ c. mashed bananas
  (approximately 4 bananas)
1 Tbsp. lemon juice
2 c. flour

1 tsp. baking soda
½ tsp. salt
½ tsp. cinnamon
½ tsp. lemon rind
½ c. chopped walnuts
  (optional)

Beat eggs well. Add margarine and sugar and cream with eggs. Add remaining ingredients. Grease 9 x 5 loaf pan. Bake at 350° for 55 minutes.

Kathy Lore

❧ MONKEY BREAD ❧

4 (approximately 10 oz.) cans
  refrigerated biscuits
¾ c. sugar

2 Tbsp. cinnamon
1 ½ sticks margarine (¾ c.)
1 c. sugar

Cut biscuits into quarters. Combine sugar and cinnamon and shake the biscuit pieces in that to coat well. Put into a Bundt pan sprayed with vegetable oil. Combine margarine and 1 cup sugar and bring to a boil. Pour over biscuits. Bake at 350° for about 35 to 40 minutes. Invert on plate and serve while warm.

Kathy Lore

❧ BANANA BREAD ❧

1 c. sugar
½ c. Crisco
2 eggs
1 ½ c. flour
2 tsp. baking powder

1 scant soda
1 c. mashed ripe bananas
½ c. nuts (optional)
pinch of salt
1 tsp. vanilla

Mix sugar, Crisco and eggs. Add remaining ingredients to mixture. Put in loaf pan (greased and floured). Bake for 1 hour in 300° oven or until toothpick comes out clean.

Betty Ann Smith

🌱 BLUEBERRY MUFFINS 🌱

2 c. flour	1 c. milk
¾ c. sugar	¾ c. oil
3 tsp. baking powder	1 egg
½ tsp. salt	2 c. frozen blueberries

Mix flour, sugar, baking powder and salt well. Add and mix the milk, oil and egg. Add/fold in 2 cups frozen blueberries. Bake at 375° for 15 to 18 minutes.
May's recipe.

Kathy Lore

🌱 STRAWBERRY NUT BREAD 🌱

2 (10 oz.) pkg. frozen strawberries	2 c. sugar
4 eggs	3 tsp. cinnamon
1 ½ c. salad oil	1 tsp. baking soda
3 c. flour	1 tsp. salt
	1 c. chopped nuts

Combine thawed strawberries, egg and oil. (Do not drain strawberries; use all.) In large bowl, combine sugar, cinnamon, baking soda, salt and nuts. Add to strawberries; mix well. Bake in two 9 x 5 loaf pans for 1 hour.

Delores Demichele

🌱 RAISIN BRAN MUFFINS 🌱

4 eggs, beaten	5 c. flour
4 c. buttermilk	1 tsp. salt
5 tsp. soda	1 c. oil
3 c. sugar	1 (15 oz.) box Raisin Bran

Refrigerate for 3 days before baking. Will keep for 3 months in fridge. Bake at 400° for 15 to 20 minutes.

Kathy Lore

STICKY ROLLS

1 c. brown sugar
½ c. corn syrup

½ c. margarine
1 c. chopped nuts (optional)

Cook first 3 ingredients until sugar is dissolved. Pour into a 9 x 3 pan. Cut 2 tubes of refrigerator biscuits in half. Dip and fully coat in a mixture of ½ cup white sugar and ¼ cup cinnamon. Place biscuits in pan, cut side down. Bake at 375° for 25 to 30 minutes.

Rita Donner

-•EXTRA RECIPES•-

YOUR FAVORITE RECIPES

Recipe   **Page Number**

Cakes, Cookies
and Desserts

Recipe Favorites

Page No.

Recipe Title:_____ _____

_____ _____

_____ _____

_____ _____

_____ _____

_____ _____

_____ _____

_____ _____

_____ _____

Family Favorites

Page No.

Recipe Title:_____ _____

_____ _____

_____ _____

_____ _____

_____ _____

Notes:_____

_____

_____

_____

CAKES, COOKIES & DESSERTS

☙ FRESH APPLE CAKE ☙

3 Tbsp. oleo
1 c. sugar
1 beaten egg
1 tsp. soda
½ tsp. cinnamon

½ tsp. nutmeg
1 tsp. vanilla
1 c. flour
3 c. chopped apples
½ c. chopped nuts

Cream sugar and oleo; add egg. Sift dry ingredients together and add. Mix well. Add apples and nuts; mix. Bake in loaf pan at 350° about 45 minutes.

Jackie Wallace

☙ WHIPPED FROSTING ☙

1 ½ c. milk
2 Tbsp. cornstarch or 3 ½
  Tbsp. flour
⅔ c. Crisco

½ c. butter or oleo
1 c. sugar
1 tsp. vanilla

Cook milk and cornstarch or flour until thick. Cool. Beat remaining ingredients with mixer, then pour in cooled paste and beat until thick enough to spread.

Jackie Wallace

☙ COOKED FROSTING ☙
(Soft and Fluffy)

5 Tbsp. flour
1 c. milk
1 c. sugar

1 c. butter and Crisco (½
  each)
1 tsp. flavoring

Boil flour and milk until thick, then cool to room temperature. Add sugar and butter/Crisco to mixture. Beat with mixer and add flavoring. (Usually need an extra tablespoon flour.) Use ½ recipe for layer cake. Can refrigerate for at least 1 month.

Barbara Fehr

🌺 PINEAPPLE CAKE 🌺

1 box angel food cake mix   1 (20 oz.) can undrained crushed pineapple

Mix cake and pineapple. Pour into ungreased 9 x 13 pan. Bake according to package directions.

🌺 FRESH APPLE CAKE 🌺

4 c. apple, peeled and chopped	1 c. nuts
2 c. sugar	2 c. flour
1 c. oil	1 tsp. soda
2 eggs, well beaten	2 Tbsp. cinnamon
1 tsp. vanilla	1 tsp. salt

Mix by hand in order listed. Pour into 9 x 12 greased cake pan or Bundt pan. Bake at 350° for 1 hour.

Sally Buck

🌺 LEMON JELLO CAKE 🌺

1 yellow cake mix	4 eggs
1 small lemon jello	1 lemon or lemon juice
1 c. boiling water	powdered sugar
¾ c. oil	

Mix lemon jello and boiling water. Cool. Add jello mixture to cake. Add oil and 1 egg at a time. Mix. Pour in Bundt pan. Bake at 350° for 40 minutes. Remove from pan. Immediately glaze over cake. I use lemon cake mix as I like lemon taste.

Sally Buck

🌿 BUTTERSCOTCH SNACK CAKE 🌿

1 (3.5 oz.) pkg. cook and
　serve butterscotch
　pudding
2 c. milk
1 (18 ¼ oz.) pkg. yellow cake
　mix

1 (11 oz.) pkg. butterscotch
　baking chips
½ c. chopped pecans or
　walnuts

In a large saucepan, combine pudding mix and milk. Bring to a boil over medium heat, stirring constantly. Remove from the heat. Stir in dry cake mix. Pour into greased 13 x 9 x 2-inch baking pan. Sprinkle with butterscotch chips and nuts. Bake at 350° for 35 to 40 minutes or until a toothpick inserted near the center comes out clean. Cool on a wire rack. Yields 12 to 16 servings.

Eileen Freeman

🌿 3 LAYER CAKE 🌿

1 box yellow cake mix
4 eggs
1 stick margarine (room
　temperature)

11 oz. can mandarin oranges
　with juice

Frosting:

9 oz. container Cool Whip

3 oz. instant vanilla pudding

Add 1 pound 4 ounce can crushed pineapple juice.
Mix cake ingredients. Pour into 3 greased layer pans. Make 3 rounds of wax paper in each pan. Bake at 325° for 20 minutes. Cool.
Blend frosting ingredients.

Rita Donner

🌿 HAWAIIAN WEDDING CAKE 🌿

2 c. flour
2 eggs, beaten
2 c. sugar
2 tsp. baking soda

1 (20 oz.) can pineapple,
　crushed
1 c. shredded coconut
1 c. nuts

Bake at 350° for 45 minutes in 9 x 12 pan. Ice while warm.

Icing:

8 oz. cream cheese
1 stick (½ c.) margarine

1 ½ c. powdered sugar
1 tsp. vanilla

Cream oleo and cheese; add vanilla. Slowly add sugar until creamy.

Harriet Lapp

❧ RHUBARB UPSIDE-DOWN CAKE ❧

5 c. rhubarb
1 (3 oz.) raspberry Jell-O
1 white cake mix

1 c. sugar
3 c. mini marshmallows
2 eggs

Cut rhubarb into ½-inch pieces. Arrange in greased 9 x 13-inch pan. Sprinkle with sugar and Jell-O. Top with marshmallows. Prepare cake as directed using 2 eggs and water. Spread batter over marshmallows. Bake at 350° for 55 minutes. Cool for 5 minutes and turn out on tray. Serve with whip cream.

Louise Johnson

❧ ECLAIR CAKE ❧

Crust:

½ c. margarine
1 c. water

1 c. flour
4 eggs

Boil margarine and water. Stir flour into mixture and cool slightly. Beat eggs into mixture 1 at a time. Spread into a 9 x 13-inch pan. Bake at 400° for 30 minutes. (This will rise and sink, leaving an eclair crust.)

Filling:

3 boxes vanilla instant pudding

1 (8 oz.) pkg. cream cheese
5 c. milk

Mix well. (I add some milk to cream cheese; blend in blender and then use whisk or mixer to blend all.) Pour into crust. Top with Cool Whip and chocolate syrup. Chill before serving.

Cindy Andrus

❧ FUDGE RICOTTA CHEESE CAKE ❧

1 ¼ c. chocolate cookie
  crumbs
3 Tbsp. margarine
32 oz. Ricotta cheese
1 ¼ c. sugar
4 eggs

½ c. unsweetened cocoa
  powder
3 Tbsp. flour
1 tsp. vanilla extract
1 c. sour cream
½ c. chopped hazelnuts or
  other nuts

Lightly grease 8 or 9-inch spring-form pan. Combine cookie crumbs and margarine; mix well and press evenly over bottom and 1-inch up sides of pan. Chill while preparing the filling.

In large bowl with electric mixer, beat Ricotta cheese at high speed, gradually blending in sugar and eggs. Reduce speed; add cocoa, flour and vanilla until blended. Add sour cream and blend until smooth. Stir in nuts. Pour mixture into crust and bake in a preheated 350° oven until the cake sets, about 1 hour and 15 to 30 minutes. Remove from oven and cool completely on wire rack. Chill in refrigerator for 8 hours or more. Remove cake from sides of pan with a knife close to pan. Can serve with whipped cream and strawberries or raspberries used for pie filling.

Agnes Billisits

❧ OUR FINEST CHEESECAKE ❧
(Makes 1 nine-inch cake.)

Crust:

1 ½ c. graham cracker
  crumbs
3 Tbsp. sugar

½ tsp. ground cinnamon
¼ c. (½ stick) sweet butter,
  melted

Filling:

3 (8 oz.) pkg. cream cheese
  (room temperature)
1 ¼ c. sugar
6 eggs, separated
1 (1 pt.) container dairy sour
  cream

⅓ c. all-purpose flour
2 tsp. vanilla
grated rind of 1 lemon
juice of ½ lemon

To make crust: Generously grease a 9 x 3-inch spring-form pan with butter. Place pan in center of a 12-inch square of aluminum foil and press foil up around side of pan. Combine graham cracker crumbs, sugar, cinnamon and melted butter in a small bowl until well blended. Press ¼ cup of crumb mixture into bottom and side of pan. Chill prepared pan while making filling. (reserve remaining crumb mixture for topping.)

To make filling: With electric mixer on low speed or with a wooden spoon, beat cream cheese in a large bowl until soft. Gradually beat in sugar until light and fluffy. Beat in egg yolks, one at a time, until well blended. Stir in sour cream, flour, vanilla, lemon rind and juice until smooth. Beat egg whites until they hold stiff peaks. Fold whites into the cheese mixture, soufflé-fashion, until well blended. Pour into prepared pan. Bake in moderate oven (350°) 1 hour and 15 minutes or until top is golden; turn off oven heat and allow cake to cool in oven for 1 hour. Remove cake from oven and allow to cool on a wire rack at room temperature. Sprinkle remaining crumbs on top. Chill overnight before serving. Dust with 10x (confectioners powdered) sugar just before serving.

Agnes Billisits

❧ DATE BART CAKE ❧

1 c. dates, cut up
1 c. boiling water
1 tsp. baking soda
1 c. sugar
½ c. butter or shortening
2 eggs
1 ⅔ c. sifted flour

1 tsp. baking soda
½ tsp. salt
1 c. crushed pineapple
2 Tbsp. pineapple syrup
6 oz. pkg. chocolate chips
½ c. chopped nuts
½ c. sugar

Cover dates with boiling water; add baking soda. Let cool. Beat sugar, eggs and shortening until light. Sift dry ingredients. Add to egg mixture, beating until blended. Fold in date mixture, pineapple and syrup. Pour batter into greased 9 x 13-inch pan. Sprinkle chocolate chips, nuts and sugar over top of batter. Bake in 350° oven for 35 to 40 minutes. Needs no frosting; whipped cream may be used.

Pat Cohick

❧ HAYSTACKS ❧

6 oz. butterscotch chips
2 tsp. salad oil

2 c. Chinese noodles
1 c. salted peanuts

Over double boiler, melt chips and oil. Mix peanuts and noodles and add to butterscotch. Drop by spoonfuls onto waxed paper.

❀ DUMP CAKE ❀

1 can cherry pie filling	1 c. melted butter
1 can crushed pineapple	1 c. chopped nuts
1 box yellow cake mix	1 c. coconut

Pour cherry pie filling into 9 x 13 cake pan, then pineapple. Sprinkle dry cake mix over pineapple. Pour melted butter over cake mix, then sprinkle nuts, then coconut. Bake at 350° for 1 hour. Top with Cool Whip when serving, if desired.

Kathy Lore

❀ LAZY DAISY CAKE ❀

Part 1:

2 eggs, well beaten	1 c. flour
1 tsp. baking powder	pinch of salt
1 c. sugar	

Part 2:

½ c. milk, heated to boiling point	1 generous Tbsp. butter
	1 tsp. vanilla

Topping:

3 Tbsp. butter	5 Tbsp. brown sugar
3 Tbsp. cream	½ c. coconut

Add Part 2 to Part 1 and bake at 350° for 30 minutes. When cake is taken from oven, spread with the topping mixture and brown slightly under the broiler. Makes a 9 x 9 cake.

Harold Yannayon

❀ CREAM CHEESE CAKE ❀

2 pkg. crescent rolls	1 egg (yolk and white
2 (8 oz.) cream cheese	separated)
1 tsp. vanilla	1 c. sugar

Spread 1 package of crescent rolls in a 9 x 13 pan. Beat egg yolk, vanilla, cream cheese and sugar. Pour over crescent roll layer. Spread second package of rolls on wax paper same size as 9 x 13 pan. Place over cream cheese mixture. Beat egg white, then spread on top layer of crescent rolls.

½ c. chopped nuts   1 tsp. vanilla
½ c. sugar

Mix. Sprinkle on top. Bake at 350° for 30 to 35 minutes.

Terry Powers

APPLE CAKE

1 stick oleo   1 tsp. nutmeg
2 c. sugar   1 tsp. soda
2 eggs   ½ tsp. salt
2 c. flour   5 c. chopped apples
1 tsp. cinnamon   1 c. nuts

Mix together oleo, sugar and eggs, then add remaining ingredients. Bake in cake pan at 350° until done.

Aunt Girlie

FRANK'S ORANGE CAKE

1 yellow cake mix   20 oz. can crushed
11 oz. can mandarin oranges,   pineapple, drained
  drained and syrup   12 oz. Cool Whip
  reserved   3 oz. pkg. instant vanilla
3 eggs   pudding
⅓ c. vegetable oil

Preheat oven to 350°. Grease and flour 2 (8 or 9-inch) cake pans. Place dry cake mix in large bowl. Add orange syrup plus however much water is required to equal 1 ⅓ cups of liquid. Add eggs and oil and beat at low speed until moistened. Add drained oranges. Beat at medium speed for 2 minutes. Pour batter into pans and bake immediately, 33 to 36 minutes for 8-inch pans, 28 to 31 minutes for 9-inch pans or until toothpick inserted in the middle of the cake comes out clean. Cool in pan on rack for 15 minutes. Remove from pan and cool completely before frosting.

CAKES, COOKIES & DESSERTS

To make frosting, mix together pineapple and Cool Whip, then slowly add the instant pudding. Beat.

Michelle Lynam

❧ BLUEBERRY COFFEE CAKE ❧

¾ c. sugar
½ c. margarine
2 eggs
½ tsp. vanilla

1 ⅔ c. flour
¼ tsp. salt
½ c. milk

Topping:

2 Tbsp. sugar

1 tsp. cinnamon

Cream sugar, margarine, eggs and vanilla thoroughly. Add flour, baking powder and salt and blend. Add to creamed mixture with milk. Mix until smooth. Fold in 1 ½ cups blueberries. Spread batter over 8-inch square pan.

Mix sugar and cinnamon and spread or sprinkle lightly over batter. Bake at 350° for 30 or 35 minutes. Cake is excellent.

Sally Fitzgerald

❧ PUMPKIN PIE CAKE ❧

1 yellow cake mix (remove 1
   c. of mix to use later)

1 stick melted margarine
   or ½ c. oil
2 beaten eggs

This mixture should be thick so mix with a fork. Press into greased 13 x 9 pan.

Filling:

1 large can pumpkin
3 eggs
½ c. brown sugar, packed

¼ c. white sugar
⅔ c. milk
1 ½ tsp. cinnamon

Mix and beat well. Spread over crust in bottom of pan.

Topping:

1 c. yellow cake mix
½ c. sugar

½ c. nuts, chopped
½ stick cold margarine

Spread crumb mixture on top of filling. Bake at 350° for 55 minutes or tested like you would a pumpkin pie with a knife. Delicious!!

Emily Gardner

🌿 1 EGG CAKE 🌿
(Great for Strawberry Shortcake.)

⅔ c. sugar	1 egg
¼ c. shortening	1 ½ c. flour
¼ tsp. salt	½ c. milk
1 tsp. vanilla	2 tsp. baking powder

Cream sugar and shortening together. Add egg and vanilla. Mix thoroughly. Combine flour, salt and baking powder. Add slowly to mixture, alternating with milk. Blend well. Place in greased 8 x 8 pan. Bake at 375° for 30 to 35 minutes.

🌿 PUMPKIN WHOOPIES 🌿

1 c. canned pumpkin	2 eggs
⅓ c. butter (soft)	½ c. milk
1 pkg. (2 layer size) spice cake mix (9 x 13 size)	

Preheat oven to 375°. Line cookie sheet with parchment paper. Mix pumpkin and butter with electric mixer until smooth. Add cake mix, eggs and milk. By heaping tablespoon, drop on cookie sheet 3-inches apart. Chill remaining batter. Bake 12 minutes. Continue until all batter is baked.

Marshmallow-Spice Filling:

½ c. butter (soft)	1 tsp. vanilla
8 oz. pkg. cream cheese (soft)	½ tsp. cinnamon
2 c. powdered sugar	½ tsp. nutmeg
½ (7 oz.) jar Marshmallow Creme	

Combine and beat until mixed well. Put filling between 2 cakes to make pies.

WHOOPIE PIES

1 c. shortening
2 c. sugar
2 egg yolks (save whites)
1 c. cocoa
2 tsp. soda
2 eggs

4 c. flour
¼ tsp. salt
2 tsp. vanilla
1 c. sour milk
1 c. hot water

Mix sugar, eggs and yolks. Add remaining ingredients. Drop by spoonfuls onto cookie sheet. Bake at 450° for 5 minutes. Spread filling between 2 cookies.

Filling:

2 unbeaten egg whites
1 tsp. vanilla
4 tsp. flour
2 tsp. powdered sugar

4 tsp. milk
1 ½ c. shortening
1 box powdered sugar

Beat together all ingredients, except box of powdered sugar, until smooth and fluffy. Then add box of sugar and beat.

DEATH BY CHOCOLATE

1 (19.8 oz. or family size) box fudge brownie mix
3 pkg. instant chocolate mousse mix (each pkg. makes four ½ cup servings; chocolate pudding may be substituted)

8 (1.4 oz.) chocolate covered toffee bars (Skor/Heath)
1 (12 oz.) container Cool Whip

Prepare and bake brownies according to package directions; let cool. Prepare chocolate mousse according to package directions. Break candy bars into small pieces in food processor or by gently tapping the wrapped bars with a hammer. Break up half the brownies into small pieces and place in the bottom of a large glass bowl or truffle dish. Cover with half the mousse, half of the candy and half of the whipped topping. Repeat layers with the remaining ingredients. Garnish with fresh strawberries, raspberries or another candy bar, broken into pieces. Enjoy!!!

Dianna Romanishin

SEE'S FUDGE

½ c. butter
1 (6 oz.) pkg. semi-sweet
   chocolate pieces
1 tsp. vanilla
2 c. sugar

1 (5 ¾ oz.) can evaporated
   milk (be sure to use the
   small can of milk)
10 marshmallows (large)
1 c. chopped nuts

Combine butter, chocolate pieces and vanilla in a medium bowl. Set aside. Place sugar, evaporated milk and marshmallows in medium saucepan. Bring to a boil over medium heat, stirring frequently. Reduce heat to low and cook 6 minutes, stirring constantly. Pour hot mixture over in bowl. Beat with electric mixer until fudge is thick and dull (this doesn't take long). Stir in nuts. Pour into lightly buttered 8-inch square baking pan. Refrigerate several hours to firm.

Betty Ann Smith

PEANUT BUTTER FUDGE

½ c. milk
2 c. sugar
1 c. peanut butter

1 Tbsp. butter
1 tsp. vanilla

Combine milk and sugar in 2-quart pan. Cook over medium heat approximately 20 minutes. Will be bubbly (don't stir). When mixture forms thread, remove from heat. Add peanut butter, butter and vanilla. Go quickly. Will set up quick. Pour into greased 9 x 9 pan. Refrigerate until cool. Enjoy!

Betty Ann Smith

PEANUT BUTTER FUDGE

1 c. peanut butter
1 c. butter

1 tsp. vanilla
1 lb. box confectioners sugar

Melt butter. Mix all ingredients.

Kathy Lore

SODA CRACKER FUDGE

42 crackers, crushed
4 c. sugar
1 c. milk
2 tsp. vanilla

7 Tbsp. peanut butter
1 c. chocolate chips (mini
   chips melt faster)

Bring sugar, milk and vanilla to a rapid boil. Boil 1 minute. Remove from heat and add peanut butter and chocolate chips. Stir until smooth. Add crackers and nuts (if desired). Mix until crackers disappear. Pour into pan and cool.

Kathy Lore

❧ NO FUDGIN' - BEST FUDGE ❧ EVER!

1 ½ tsp. + ¾ c. butter (no substitutions!), divided
1 (14 oz.) can condensed milk
3 Tbsp. milk
1 (12 oz.) pkg. semi-sweet chocolate chips
1 (11 ½ oz.) pkg. milk chocolate chips
1 (10 oz.) pkg. peanut butter chips
1 c. butterscotch chips
1 (7 oz.) jar marshmallow cream
½ tsp. almond extract
1 c. chopped walnuts or pecans

Line 13 x 9 x 2 pan with foil and grease with the 1 ½ teaspoons butter. In a large heavy saucepan, melt the remaining butter over low heat. Add next 5 ingredients. Cook, stirring constantly, until smooth. Remove from heat; stir in butterscotch chips, marshmallow cream and extracts until well blended. Add nuts. Spread into pan and chill until set. Lift out of pan; remove foil and cut into squares. Store in the refrigerator. Makes about 4 ½ pounds.

Betty Ann Smith

❧ PECAN CARAMEL CANDIES ❧

63 miniature pretzels
1 (13 oz.) pkg. Rolo candies
63 pecan halves

Line baking sheet with foil. Place pretzels on foil. Top each pretzel with candy. Bake at 250° for 4 minutes. Immediately place pecan on top. Cool slightly. Refrigerate for 10 minutes.

Eileen Freeman

❧ NO BAKE COOKIES ❧

1 c. butter
4 c. sugar
1 c. milk
3 to 4 Tbsp. cocoa
½ tsp. salt
1 c. peanut butter
2 tsp. vanilla
6 c. quick oats

Bring first 5 ingredients to a rapid boil and let boil for 4 ½ minutes. Remove from fire and add peanut butter, vanilla and oats. Drop by teaspoonfuls onto waxed paper. Have peanut butter and oats ready before starting as they will harden fast.

Kathy Lore

❧ BOILED OATMEAL COOKIES ❧

2 c. sugar
½ c. milk
¼ c. oleo (butter)
3 Tbsp. cocoa

1 tsp. vanilla
½ c. peanut butter
½ c. nuts
3 c. quick oats

Boil sugar and milk 1 minute. Mix quickly; drop on wax paper.

❧ CHOCOLATE CHIP COOKIES ❧

2 c. butter
2 c. sugar
2 c. brown sugar
4 eggs
3 tsp. vanilla
4 c. flour

5 c. ground oatmeal (put in blender or food processor)
2 tsp. salt
2 tsp. soda
2 tsp. baking powder
24 oz. chocolate chips
3 c. crushed walnuts

Cream butter, sugar, brown sugar, eggs and vanilla. Roll into small balls and bake on ungreased cookie sheets at 350° for 5 ½ minutes.

Kathy Lore

❧ PEANUT BUTTER COOKIES ❧

½ c. sugar (white)
½ c. brown sugar
½ c. butter or margarine
½ c. peanut butter (smooth or crunchy)

1 egg
1 ¼ c. flour
½ tsp. baking soda
¾ tsp. soda
¼ tsp. salt

Mix sugars, butter or margarine, peanut butter and egg. Add remaining ingredients to mixture. Chill dough. Roll into balls; use flour on fork to make indenture on cookies on ungreased cookie sheet. Bake in 375° oven 10 to 12 minutes. Makes approximately 3 dozen.

Betty Ann Smith

❧ SNICKERDOODLES ❧

1 ½ c. sugar
½ c. butter or margarine
½ c. shortening
2 eggs

2 ¾ c. flour
2 tsp. cream of tartar
1 tsp. soda
¼ tsp. salt

Mix together sugar, butter or margarine, shortening and eggs. Add remaining ingredients. Refrigerate dough in wax paper for ½ to 1 hour. Roll into balls. Roll into mixture of 3 tablespoons sugar and 1 tablespoon cinnamon. Cook 8 to 10 minutes on ungreased cookie sheet at 375° to 400° in oven. Balls will puff up, then collapse into cookie.

Betty Ann Smith

❧ RUSSIAN TEA BALLS ❧

1 c. butter or margarine
½ c. confectioners sugar
2 ¼ c. flour

¾ c. walnuts, ground
1 tsp. vanilla
¼ tsp. salt

Mix together butter or margarine and confectioners sugar. Add remaining ingredients. Chill dough ½ to 1 hour. Roll into balls on ungreased cookie sheet. Cook in 400° oven 10 to 12 minutes or until brown. Cool, then take brown bag and put 1 cup confectioners sugar. Put 4 or 5 balls in bag and slightly flour with sugar. Can repeat again to make better taste.

Betty Ann Smith

❧ PEANUT BUTTER NO BAKE ❧ COOKIES

2 c. sugar
½ c. butter
½ c. milk

5 Tbsp. peanut butter (plain or chunky)
1 tsp. vanilla
3 c. oatmeal

Boil sugar, butter and milk for 4 minutes. Add peanut butter and mix, then add vanilla and oatmeal. Mix and drop by spoonfuls onto waxed paper. Let cool.

SOFT SUGAR COOKIES

1 ½ c. sugar
1 c. butter
2 eggs
1 tsp. lemon extract

4 c. flour
2 tsp. baking powder
½ c. canned evaporated milk

Cream together sugar and butter; add eggs and beat well. Alternate 2 cups flour and ¼ cup milk, then add rest. Chill dough. Roll out dough on floured board approximately ¼ to ½-inch thickness. Cut desired shapes. Bake at 350° for 10 minutes or 8 minutes at 450°. Remove from oven when cookies are just lightly brown on bottoms. Ovens and times will vary.

Kathy Lore

HOLLY COOKIES

½ c. margarine
3 c. miniature marshmallows

1 tsp. vanilla
¼ tsp. green food coloring

Melt down and pour over 2 ½ to 3 cups any flake cereal (Corn Flakes, Wheaties, etc.). Mix and drop by teaspoon onto wax paper. Put 3 red cinnamon dots on each to resemble holly.

Kathy Lore

BUTTERBALL COOKIES

3 ¾ c. flour
¾ tsp. salt
1 c. confectioners sugar
1 ½ c. soft butter

4 Tbsp. milk (= ¼ c.)
1 ½ c. chopped walnuts
3 tsp. vanilla

Mix all ingredients. Roll into balls about 1-inch. Bake at 300° for 20 minutes. Roll in confectioners sugar while hot and once after they are cooled.

Kathy Lore

NO BAKE FUDGE COOKIES

2 c. sugar
1 stick oleo (½ c.)
½ c. milk
½ c. Nestle's hot cocoa mix

3 c. oats
½ c. peanut butter
1 tsp. vanilla

CAKES, COOKIES & DESSERTS

Mix first 4 ingredients together in a big saucepan. Boil for 1 minute after it comes to a rolling boil. Remove from heat and add oats, peanut butter and vanilla. Drop by teaspoonfuls on wax paper and let cool.

Helpful Hint: Have oats and peanut butter already measured out and ready as cookies will start to harden in saucepan very quickly.

⚜ MACAROONS ⚜

1 ½ c. rice crispy cereal
1 ¼ c. flaked coconut
2 egg whites

3 Tbsp. sugar
⅛ tsp. almond extract

In small bowl, combine all ingredients. Use damp spoon or fingers. Shape into 1 ½-inch pile on a parchment paper-lined cookie sheet. Bake at 300° for 20 to 25 minutes or until edges are lightly brown. Remove from pan and cool on wire racks. Yields about 2 dozen.

Martha Tomlinson

⚜ GRAHAM CRACKER TOFFEE ⚜
COOKIES

graham crackers
2 sticks butter (regular not
   unsalted)

½ c. sugar
walnuts

Line a large cookie sheet with aluminum foil, shiny side down. Fill with single layer of crackers. Bring butter and sugar to a full boil. Boil for 2 minutes. Pour over crackers (spread with a wooden spoon) and sprinkle with chopped nuts. Bake at 350° for 10 minutes. Remove and cool on racks. Put a brown paper bag or newspaper under racks, as cookies will drip. Makes easier clean up. Enjoy.

Mary Ellen Carrick

⚜ NUTMEG COOKIES ⚜

2 c. brown sugar
1 c. water
1 c. lard

2 tsp. cream of tartar
1 tsp. baking soda
1 ½ tsp. nutmeg

Just put in enough flour to be able to roll dough. Bake at 350° until done.

Delores Demichele

🌿 HAMBURGER COOKIES 🌿

1 box Nilla vanilla wafers
1 pkg. Keebler fudge
   grasshoppers

1 tube gel icing (red)
1 tube gel icing (yellow)

Lay 2 rows of wafer cookies and 1 row Keebler cookies. Squeeze red icing on one side, then yellow icing. Press 3 cookies together. Brush egg whites on top and sprinkle with sesame seeds.

You can add green jimmies for lettuce or color coconut with green food coloring. Place on red or yellow icing before putting together.

Carol Bohman

🌿 PIZZELLES 🌿

12 eggs
3 ½ c. sugar
2 c. melted margarine (not
   hot)

1 tsp. pure anise or 4 tsp.
   vanilla
1 tsp. salt
6 c. flour

Mix eggs, sugar and margarine. Add anise or vanilla, salt and flour. Chill dough overnight. Drop by teaspoonfuls onto heated pizzelle iron. Cook to desired color.

Kathy Lore

🌿 EASY-TIME HOLIDAY SQUARES 🌿

1 ½ c. sugar
1 c. butter or oleo
4 eggs
2 c. flour

1 Tbsp. lemon extract or
   juice
1 can cherry pie filling

Gradually add sugar to butter on medium speed until fluffy. Add eggs one at a time. Beat well after each. Add flour and lemon at low speed. Pour batter into well-greased pan (9 x 13) and place heaping tablespoonful filling in each square. Bake at 350° for 25 to 30 minutes. Dust top with powdered sugar.

Barbara Fehr

RAISIN APPLE BETTY

2 cans apple pie filling   ½ tsp. cinnamon (per layer)
instant raisin oatmeal spice

Spray fluted pan with Pam or cooking spray. Layer apple pie filling, then instant raisin/oatmeal and cinnamon until gone. Put 3 slices of butter on top. Cook at 400° for 30 to 40 minutes.

Richard Smith

PINEAPPLE SQUARES
(Makes: Depends on size of squares.)

1 Duncan Hines deluxe cake mix

Follow directions. Bake in large jelly roll pan 18 to 20 minutes. Cool!

2 cans crushed pineapple (1   2 ¾ c. milk
    lb. 4 oz.)   1 (8 oz.) cream cheese,
1 (6 oz.) instant vanilla   softened
    pudding   1 (8 oz.) container Cool Whip

Drain pineapple. Spread on cake. Mix at low speed the pudding with milk for 2 minutes. Blend in cream cheese and Cool Whip. Spread on top of pineapple topping. Add crushed nuts and coconut, if desired. Refrigerate.

Dianna Romanishin

APPLE OAT CRUMBLE

8 c. apples, sliced   1 tsp. cinnamon
1 tsp. grated orange rind   ½ tsp. nutmeg
⅔ c. orange juice   ¼ tsp. salt
1 c. sugar   6 Tbsp. margarine
⅔ c. oatmeal   12 Tbsp. Cool Whip
½ c. flour

Preheat oven to 375°. Place apples in an 8-inch square baking pan and sprinkle with orange rind and juice. Combine sugar and next 5 ingredients in a bowl. Mix well. Cut margarine with a pastry blender or 2 knives until it resembles coarse meal. Sprinkle mixture over apple slices. Bake at 375° for 40 minutes or until apples are tender and topping is lightly browned. Top with whipped topping. Yields 6 servings.

Rita Donner

❧ LEMON BARS ❧

1 box angel food cake mix   1 (22 oz.) can lemon pie
                             filling

Bake in 9 x 13 pan 25 to 30 minutes at 350°.
Option: Can add ½ cup coconut.
Cut into bars.

❧ FAMOUS 1 BOWL BROWNIES ❧
(Takes exactly 3 minutes to assemble.)

1 stick butter   5 Tbsp. Hershey's cocoa
1 c. brown sugar   1 tsp. vanilla
½ c. white flour   1 beaten egg

Melt butter in oven (8 x 8-inch pan). Add remaining ingredients. Stir together and bake in 325° oven for ½ hour. If you want to frost, do so right after baking:

1 c. confectioners sugar   1 tsp. vanilla
2 Tbsp. Hershey's cocoa   boiling water (enough for
2 Tbsp. melted butter   spreading consistency)

Gloria Love

❧ QUICK AND EASY COOKIE BARS ❧

1 pkg. graham crackers   2 eggs, beaten
  (about 1 ⅔ c.)   1 Tbsp. water
½ c. flour   1 tsp. vanilla
½ tsp. soda   1 pkg. chocolate chips
½ c. melted oleo   1 c. chopped nuts
½ c. brown sugar

Mix flour, graham crackers and soda together. Mix in remaining ingredients. Bake at 350° in a cake pan until done.

Dorothy Lytle

🌺 PUMPKIN BARS 🌺

2 c. sugar	2 c. Bisquick baking mix
½ c. oil	2 tsp. cinnamon
1 can pumpkin	½ c. raisins
4 eggs	

Beat sugar, oil, pumpkin and eggs together. Stir in baking mix and raisins. Grease cake or jelly roll pan. Bake at 350° for 25 to 30 minutes.

Dorothy Lytle

🌺 TUTTI FRUTTI LEMON DELIGHT 🌺

1 (8 ¾ oz.) can pineapple tidbits with juice	½ c. coconut
1 (11 oz.) can mandarin oranges with juice	2 tsp. lemon juice
1 (17 oz.) can fruit cocktail with juice	3 ¾ oz. pkg. instant lemon pudding
	2 bananas

Combine all ingredients except lemon pudding and bananas. Sprinkle instant lemon pudding over top. Stir lightly to combine. Chill and just before serving, add 2 sliced bananas. Makes 10 servings. Can be served in sherbet dishes.

Pat Cohick

🌺 ORANGE PINEAPPLE DELIGHT 🌺

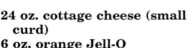

24 oz. cottage cheese (small curd)	2 (20 oz.) cans pineapple chunks or tidbits
6 oz. orange Jell-O	1 (8 oz.) Cool Whip
2 (11 oz.) cans Mandarin oranges	

Put cottage cheese in a large bowl. Sprinkle Jell-O powder over the cheese and stir. Drain the juice from the oranges and pineapple; then add to cheese mixture along with Cool Whip. Mix well; cover and chill until ready to serve. That's all!! (Can be easily reduced to half recipe for smaller gatherings.)

Louise Yannayon

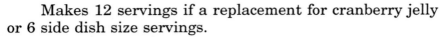

CRAN-APPLE CASSEROLE

Makes 12 servings if a replacement for cranberry jelly or 6 side dish size servings.

4 to 6 cored, peeled and
  cubed apples
2 c. cranberries
1 ¼ c. sugar
⅓ c. flour

¼ c. melted butter/margarine
⅓ c. flour
⅔ c. brown sugar
1 ¼ c. oatmeal
nuts (optional)

Combine apples, cranberries, sugar and ⅓ cup flour and place in greased casserole (2-quart minimum). Top with following mixture: butter/margarine, ⅓ cup flour, brown sugar, oatmeal and nuts. Bake at 350° for 1 hour or until hot and bubbly. (Cranberries will pop.)

CINNAMON APPLE CRISP

6 to 8 medium apples,
  peeled, cored and thinly
  sliced
1 c. water
1 c. oats
1 pkg. large moist white
  cake mix

1 c. firmly packed light
  brown sugar
½ c. butter or margarine,
  melted
1 tsp. ground cinnamon
frozen whipped topping,
  thawed (optional)
ice cream (optional)

Preheat oven to 350°. Arrange apple slices in greased 13 x 9 x 2-inch pan. Pour water over. Combine oats, cake mix, brown sugar, melted butter and cinnamon. Stir until well blended. (Mixture will be crumbly.) Sprinkle crumb mixture over apples. Bake at 350° for 50 to 55 minutes or until lightly browned and bubbly. Serve warm with topping or ice cream. Makes 12 servings.

FAVORITE BROWNIES

¾ c. flour
¼ c. baking soda
¾ c. sugar
⅓ c. butter
2 Tbsp. water

1 pkg. chocolate chips
1 tsp. vanilla
2 large eggs
½ c. chopped walnuts

Whisk together flour and soda. In small saucepan, melt butter, sugar and water. Bring to boil and remove from heat.

CAKES, COOKIES & DESSERTS

Stir in ½ of chocolate chips until melted. In large bowl, mix batter with 2 eggs, gradually stirring in flour, nuts and chocolate chips. Bake at 325° in well-greased 9-inch square pan for 40 minutes. Double recipe if you have to share!

Janey Morell

❧ PUMPKIN PIE DESSERT SQUARES ❧

1 pkg. yellow cake mix
½ c. butter or margarine,
   melted

1 egg

Filling:

3 c. (1 lb. 14 oz. can)
   pumpkin pie mix

2 eggs
⅔ c. milk

Topping:

1 c. reserved cake mix
¼ c. sugar

1 tsp. cinnamon
¼ c. butter or margarine

Grease bottom of 13 x 9-inch pan. Reserve 1 cup cake mix for topping. Combine remaining cake mix, butter and egg. Press into pan.

Prepare filling by combining all ingredients until smooth. Pour over crust.

For topping, combine all ingredients. Sprinkle over filling. Bake at 350° for 45 to 50 minutes or until knife inserted near center comes out clean.

Tip: For use with 1 pound can solid pack pumpkin, add 2 ½ teaspoons pumpkin pie spices and ½ cup firmly packed brown sugar.

Judy Nass

❧ APPLE CRISP ❧

4 c. peeled, cored and sliced
   apples
¾ c. quick oats
¾ c. firmly packed brown
   sugar

½ c. unsifted unbleached
   flour
1 tsp. cinnamon
½ c. butter or margarine,
   softened

Place apples in 9-inch square pan. Combine remaining ingredients in mixing bowl and sprinkle over apples. Bake at 350° for 40 to 45 minutes, until topping is golden brown.

Kathy Lore

BULK BROWNIE MIX

5 c. sugar
3 c. all-purpose flour

1 (8 oz.) can baking cocoa
1 tsp. salt

Mix ingredients and store in an airtight container in a cool dry place for up to 6 months. Makes approximately 10 cups of mix.

To make brownies from mix:

2 c. Brownie Mix
½ c. butter or margarine,
   melted

2 eggs, lightly beaten
1 Tbsp. water
½ tsp. vanilla

Mix ingredients and pour into a greased 8 x 8 pan. Bake at 350° for 25 to 30 minutes or until a toothpick comes out clean when inserted in middle. Cool on wire rack.

Kathy Lore

RAISINS AND RICE PUDDING

3 ½ c. fat-free milk
1 c. uncooked instant rice
1 (4.6 oz.) pkg. cook vanilla
   pudding mix

1 c. raisins
½ tsp. ground cinnamon

In a saucepan, bring milk and rice to a boil over medium heat. Whisk in pudding mix. Cook and stir for 1 minute or until thickened. Remove from heat; add raisins. Cover and wait 5 minutes. Pour into large dessert bowl or 6 individual bowls. Sprinkle cinnamon over top of pudding.

Martha Tomlinson

CAKES, COOKIES & DESSERTS

Beverages, Microwave
and Misc.

Recipe Favorites

Page No.

Recipe Title:_____

_____ _____

_____ _____

_____ _____

_____ _____

_____ _____

_____ _____

_____ _____

_____ _____

_____ _____

_____ _____

Family Favorites

Page No.

Recipe Title:_____

_____ _____

_____ _____

_____ _____

_____ _____

_____ _____

Notes:_____

_____

_____

_____

BEVERAGES, MICROWAVE & MISCELLANEOUS

❧ CAPPUCCINO PUNCH ❧

½ c. sugar
¼ c. instant coffee granules
1 c. boiling water
2 qt. milk

1 qt. vanilla ice cream, softened
1 qt. chocolate ice cream, softened

In a small bowl, combine the sugar and coffee; stir in boiling water until dissolved. Cover and refrigerate until chilled. Just before serving, pour coffee mixture into a 1-gallon punch bowl. Stir in milk. Add scoops of ice cream; stir until melted. Yield: about 1 gallon.

Louise Johnson

❧ SPICED TEA ❧

1 jar instant tea mix
1 container lemonade (juice mix, same as Kool-Aid type)

1 container Tang
1 (2 ½ oz.) jar cinnamon nutmeg/allspice to taste

❧ HOT CHOCOLATE ❧

1 large box Nestle Quik or Hershey's
1 lb. powdered sugar
1 large jar coffee creamer

1 bag miniature marshmallows
1 box powdered milk (approximately 1 lb. box)

Mix together and store in airtight container. Use desired amount, mixed with hot water.

RANCH CHICKEN SALAD SANDWICH SPREAD

A great way to use left over chicken. Chunks of cooked chicken off the bone can be substituted.

2 cooked, cooled and
  seasoned boneless chicken
  breasts
1 small onion

2 stalks celery
¾ c. Ranch dressing
½ tsp. black pepper

Shred chicken, onions and celery in food processor. Add pepper; stir in Ranch dressing.

Chuck Crouch

SAUSAGE AND EGG CASSEROLE
(5 to 6 Servings)

6 eggs, beaten
2 c. milk
2 slices bread

1 lb. mild cooked drained
  sausage
1 c. grated Cheddar cheese

Mix eggs and milk. Break bread into bite-sized pieces and add. Stir in sausage and Cheddar. Pour into greased casserole (I use 9 x 9-inch Corning pan). Refrigerate over-night. Bake at 350° for 45 minutes or until done.

Cindy Andrus

APPLE FRENCH TOAST

1 loaf French bread, sliced
  1 ½-inch thick
8 eggs
3 c. milk
¼ c. sugar

1 tsp. vanilla
5 Granny Smith apples
½ c. sugar
2 tsp. cinnamon
2 Tbsp. butter

Place bread in greased 9 x 13 pan. Mix well the eggs, milk, ½ cup sugar and vanilla. Pour half of egg mixture over bread. Slice apples over bread. Pour remaining egg mixture over apples. Mix ½ cup sugar and cinnamon and sprinkle over top, then dot with butter. Bake at 350° for 35 minutes. Let stand for 5 to 10 minutes before serving.

Tammie Wadding

❧ EASY CHEESE AND BACON ❧ QUICHE

A press-in-the-pan Bisquick® crust? Serving quiche has just become extra easy.

Prep Time: 15 minutes. Start to Finish: 55 minutes. Makes 8 servings.

1 ¼ c. original Bisquick® mix
¼ c. butter or margarine, softened
2 Tbsp. boiling water
1 (6 oz.) pkg. sliced Canadian bacon, chopped
1 c. shredded Swiss cheese (4 oz.)

4 medium green onions, thinly sliced (¼ c.)
1 ½ c. half and half
3 eggs
½ tsp. salt
¼ tsp. ground red pepper (cayenne)

Heat oven to 400°. Grease bottom and side of 9-inch pie plate with shortening. Stir Bisquick and butter until blended. Add boiling water; stir vigorously until soft dough forms. Press dough in bottom and up side of pie plate, forming edge on rim of plate. Sprinkle bacon, cheese and onions over crust. In medium bowl, beat half and half, eggs, salt and red pepper with spoon until blended. Pour into crust. Bake 35 to 40 minutes or until edge is golden brown and center is set.

High Altitude (3500 to 6500 feet): Heat oven to 375°.

Lee Ann Arble

❧ TURKEY SAUSAGE QUICHE ❧

Press a Bisquick® mix crust in a pie plate; fill it with a quick-mix egg filling and you'll have an oven-ready quiche.

Prep Time: 20 minutes. Start to Finish: 1 hour and 5 minutes. Makes 6 servings.

1 ¼ c. original Bisquick® mix
¼ c. butter or margarine, softened
2 Tbsp. boiling water
1 c. shredded Italian-style cheese blend (4 oz.)
1 c. cooked turkey sausage

4 medium green onions, sliced (¼ c.)
1 ½ c. half and half
3 eggs
1 tsp. chopped fresh basil leaves
¼ tsp. ground red pepper (cayenne)

Heat oven to 400°. Spray 9-inch glass pie plate with cooking spray. In small bowl, stir Bisquick mix and butter until blended. Add boiling water; stir vigorously until soft dough forms. Press dough on bottom and up side of pie plate, forming edge on rim of pie plate. Sprinkle cheese, sausage and onions over crust. In small bowl, beat half and half and eggs with fork or wire whisk; stir in basil and red pepper. Pour into crust. Bake 30 to 35 minutes or until knife inserted in center comes out clean. Let stand 10 minutes before serving.

High Altitude (3500 to 6500 feet): Decrease butter to 2 tablespoons. Bake 38 to 42 minutes.

Lee Ann Arble

❧ EGG CASSEROLE ❧

Assemble the night before and refrigerate covered overnight.

5 to 8 slices cubed bread	4 to 6 eggs, beaten
8 oz. shredded Cheddar cheese	½ tsp. dry mustard
	2 c. milk
½ lb. bacon, ham or sausage, cut in small pieces	½ tsp. salt
	½ tsp. red pepper

Grease 9 x 12 glass baking dish. Layer bread, cheese and meat. (Optional: Add onion, peppers, mushrooms, hot peppers.) Beat remaining ingredients and pour over layers. Cover and refrigerate overnight. Bake, uncovered, in 350° oven for 45 minutes.

Gail Sollman

❧ HIDDEN VALLEY RANCH OYSTER CRACKERS ❧

16 oz. plain oyster crackers	¼ tsp. lemon pepper
1 pkg. Hidden Valley Ranch buttermilk recipe salad dressing mix	1 tsp. dill weed
	¼ tsp. garlic powder
	1 c. salad oil

Combine Ranch mix and oil. Add dill weed, garlic powder and lemon pepper. Pour over crackers; stir to coat. Place in 250° oven for 15 to 20 minutes.

❧ BREAKFAST EGG SKILLET ❧

1 Tbsp. oil
2 c. frozen shredded hash browns
6 eggs, beaten
1 (2.1 oz.) pkg. ready to serve bacon, cut into ½-inch pieces
⅓ c. diced green onion
chopped tomatoes (for garnish)
⅓ c. shredded sharp cheese

Heat oil in medium nonstick skillet on medium-high. Add potatoes; cook 8 to 10 minutes, until brown. Spread evenly; mix eggs, bacon, onions, salt and pepper in small bowl. Pour over potatoes. Reduce heat. Cover and cook 10 minutes, until eggs are set. Remove from heat. Sprinkle with cheese. Garnish with chopped tomatoes and additional onions, if desired. Cut into wedges. Makes 6 servings.

Barbara Fehr

❧ PLAY DOH ❧

½ c. salt
½ c. hot water
¼ c. cold water
½ c. cornstarch

Mix salt and hot water. (Add a drop of food coloring if you want.) Boil. Mix cornstarch into cold water until there are no lumps. Add to salt mixture. Cook over low heat about 1 minute. Remove and knead. Store in plastic container or zip bag. Great winter day activity.

Janey Morell

❧ BARBEQUE HAM SANDWICH ❧

1 lb. chopped ham
½ bottle ketchup
1 Tbsp. brown sugar
1 Tbsp. red jelly
½ tsp. dry mustard
dash of salt and pepper
1 Tbsp. vinegar
1 Tbsp. water

Simmer 1 hour.

Eileen Freeman

❧ CAMP WLD SLOPPY JOES ❧

1 lb. ground beef
1 onion, finely chopped
3 Tbsp. brown sugar
3 Tbsp. mustard
¾ c. ketchup
1 tsp. Worcestershire sauce
½ tsp. chili powder
1 tsp. salt
½ tsp. pepper

Panfry ground beef and onion until well cooked. Add remaining ingredients and simmer for 15 minutes on low heat. Serves 4.

Janey Morell

❧ SLOPPY JOES ❧

1 lb. beef
1 small onion
¼ c. white vinegar
¾ c. brown sugar
½ c. water
2 Tbsp. ketchup
1 Tbsp. mustard
1 Tbsp. Worcestershire sauce
dash of chili powder

Brown beef and onion. Add remaining ingredients to meat. Simmer for 1 to 2 hours. Add cornstarch to thicken if needed.

Sharon L. Williams
Leigh Gigliotti's Mom

❧ MOM'S HAM BAR B Q SANDWICHES
(About 8)

1 c. catsup
⅓ c. brown sugar
½ tsp. dry mustard
1 Tbsp. vinegar
½ tsp. nutmeg
½ c. water
1 lb. chipped chopped ham

Simmer 20 minutes.

Cindy Andrus

❧ BBQ BEEF SANDWICHES ❧
(Crock-pot Recipe)

1 ½ lb. cubed stew meat
1 ½ lb. cubed pork
2 c. finely chopped onion
3 finely chopped green
   peppers
1 (6 oz.) can tomato paste
½ c. packed brown sugar
¼ c. chili powder or to taste
2 tsp. salt
1 tsp. dry mustard
2 tsp. Worcestershire sauce
12 (6-inch) hard rolls

Combine all ingredients except rolls in crock-pot. After approximately 8 hours, use a wire whisk to stir the mixture until meat is well shredded. Line rolls with lettuce; spoon on mixture and top with chopped tomato.

Gail Sollman

MINI MEAT LOAVES

2 lb. meat loaf mix (ground beef, pork and veal)
2 slices torn white bread
½ c. milk
½ c. seasoned bread crumbs
2 Tbsp. parsley flakes
1 egg
1 Tbsp. spicy brown mustard
2 Tbsp. ketchup

Soak bread in milk, then add bread crumbs, parsley, egg, mustard and ketchup. Season to taste with onion and garlic salt. Mix in ground meat. Shape into small loaves and add to a 9 x 13-inch baking dish. Make a small well on the top of each loaf with the back of a spoon. Top with a mixture of 2 tablespoons ketchup, 1 tablespoon mustard and 1 tablespoon brown sugar. Cover with plastic wrap and cook in microwave for 15 minutes on Medium-high. Makes 8 mini loaves.

Janey Morell

--•EXTRA RECIPES•--

Recipe   Page Number

INDEX OF RECIPES

Breads, Rolls & Pastries

Cakes, Cookies & Desserts

Beverages, Microwave & Miscellaneous

LIST OF CONTRIBUTORS

– S –

– T –

– W –

– Y –

Thank you for purchasing this fundraising cookbook

Your generous purchase will help this group raise needed funds. If you belong to a group that needs to raise funds, a personalized cookbook with local recipes is a proven, dignified way to meet your fundraising goals. As a special thank you for your purchase, Fundcraft would like to give you free access to our ONE MILLION RECIPE database, the largest collection of recipes on the web. If you complete and mail the postage paid card below, we will send you a personal identification number that will allow you immediate access to the recipe database. It's completely free. No obligation. Nothing to join. Just One Million Recipes For You To Enjoy!

YES! Please send me a personal identification number to access your One Million Recipe database.
Your e-mail and home address required.

☐ I am also interested in raising funds for my organization. Please send me a free fundraising cookbook information kit.

Organization _____

Name _____

Address _____

City _____ State _____ Zip _____

Home Phone _____

E-mail _____

You collect the recipes…Fundcraft will do the rest!

3745H-04

WE HAVE THE RECIPE FOR SUCCESSFUL FUNDRAISING!

Publish Your Own Cookbook

Request our free step-by-step information packet that will guide you through our proven cookbook program. It's easy to turn recipes into a very profitable fundraising cookbook with our "Recipes for Success" catalog.

It's easy to start your own cookbook program and earn $500-$25,000 for your church, club or group.

Fast :: Fill out and mail the postage-paid card.

Faster :: Call a customer service representative at 1-800-351-7822.

Fastest :: Request free material at www.fundcraft.com 24 hours a day.

You collect the recipes...Fundcraft will do the rest!

ORGANIZATION_____

NAME _____

ADDRESS _____

CITY_____ STATE _____ ZIP _____

PHONE (_____) _____

EMAIL _____

Cooking Hints & Tips

• Keep a recipe card upright by placing it in the tines of a fork and putting the fork handle in a glass.

• To keep a recipe book or card clean, place it under an upside-down glass pie plate. The curved bottom also magnifies the print.

• Use a photo album as a recipe book. Each time you cut a recipe out of a magazine, place it in one of the album's plastic sleeves.

• Glue an envelope to the inside of the front cover of your 'favorite' cookbook to hold new recipe cards or recipe clippings.

• Before you start baking or cooking, keep a plastic bag handy to slip over your hand when the phone rings.

• If butter is used in place of vegetable shortening, the amount of butter should be at least 1/4 more than the amount of shortening.

• It is best to cream butter by itself before adding the sugar.

• When a chocolate cake requires greasing and flouring the pans, try using cocoa instead of flour. When the cake is done, there will be no white flour residue on your cake and it adds flavor.

• Before measuring honey or other sticky ingredients, dip your spoon in oil.

• Put cold oil in a hot pan so the food won't stick.

• Add a pinch of baking soda to your frosting and the frosting will stay moist and prevent cracking.

• When you boil water, place a lid on the pot and the water will come to a boil in a shorter period of time– saving at least 10 minutes.

• To keep dough from sticking to your rolling pin, cover it with a clean stockinette.

• For shiny pie crusts, brush the crust lightly with milk.

• For sugary pie crusts, moisten the crust lightly with water or beaten egg whites, then sprinkle with sugar.

• Never salt food to be fried– it will draw moisture to the surface and cause spattering in the hot oil.

• Before heating the fat when deep fat frying, add one tablespoon white vinegar to minimize the amount of fat absorbed by the frying food. The food will taste less greasy.

• Sugar can be powdered by pounding it in a large mortar or rolling it on a paste-board with a rolling pin. It should be made very fine and always sifted.

Cooking Hints & Tips

• No more slow cooker mess— Before you start the recipe, place a turkey size browning bag in your cooker and put the ingredients inside the bag. After serving your dinner, just take the bag out and throw it away.

• Here's a neat casserole trick: When you are baking a covered casserole, keep your dish and oven neat by propping the lid open just a bit with a toothpick. This will prevent the casserole from bubbling over.

• Use double-thick paper towels to place over cooling rack to keep the rack from making imprints into the cake while cooling.

• Use one 3" pan instead of 2" layer pans for a higher cake— more cake less work. Slice lengthwise for layers.

• To make any home-made or boxed chocolate cake recipe moist and fluffier, add a spoonful of vinegar to the dry ingredients. You'll be amazed at the difference.

• Dip your icing spatula in hot water and dry with a paper towel. The heat from the water will melt the oil in the icing making it smoother.

• When you need a cake cooled and out of the pan quickly, place a cold wet towel or paper towels under the pan.

• Out of icing for your cup cakes? Just pop a marshmallow on top of each cup cake for about a minute before they come out of the oven. It will make a delicious, instant gooey frosting.

• Use dental floss to cut cakes, especially delicate, sticky ones that tend to adhere to a knife.

• Extend the shelf life of your home-made or store-bought cakes, by storing a half apple with them.

• Store a few lumps of sugar with your cheese to prevent it from molding.

• Apple sauce is a great fat substitute for low fat baking. Simply substitute half the fat in a recipe with an equal measure of applesauce.

• Disinfect your kitchen sponges by placing them in the microwave for 60 seconds.

• Peeling apples, pears and potatoes in cold, slightly salted water, will help keep them from turning brown.

• If soup tastes very salty, a raw piece of potato placed in the pot will absorb the salt.

• You can cut a meringue pie cleanly by coating both sides of a knife lightly with butter.

Napkin Folding

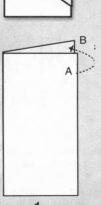

CANDLE

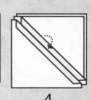

Candle Fold Instructions:
1. Fold into triangle, point at top.
2. Turn lower edge up about 1".
3. Turn over, folded edge down.
4. Roll tightly from left to right.
5. Tuck in corner. Stand upright.

DIAGONAL STRIPE

Diagonal Stripe Fold Instructions:
1. Fold edge A to edge B.
2. Fold edge A to edge B. Loose edges at top.
3. Roll down the top flap.
4. Roll down the second flap
5. Roll down the third flap
6. Fold sides back as pictured.

1

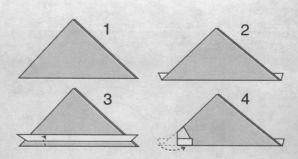

2

3

4

5

6

Table Settings

FORMAL TABLE SETTING

1. Napkin
2. Salad fork
3. Dinner fork
4. Dessert fork
5. Bread-and-butter plate, with spreader
6. Dinner plate
7. Dinner knife
8. Teaspoon
9. Teaspoon
10. Soup spoon
11. Cocktail fork
12. Water glass
13. Red-wine glass
14. White-wine glass
15. Coffee cup and saucer

GENERAL TABLE SETTING

1. Napkin
2. Salad fork
3. Dinner fork
4. Bread-and-butter plate
5. Salad plate
6. Dinner plate
7. Dinner knife
8. Teaspoon
9. Soup spoon
10. Water glass
11. Wine glass

- Don't put out utensils that won't ever be used.

- Bring the coffee cup and saucer to the table with the dessert.

Cooking Hints & Tips

MICROWAVE SHORTCUTS

TOASTING NUTS–Place 1/2 cup of nuts in a 2-cup measure. Micro-cook, uncovered, on 100% power about 3 minutes or until toasted, stirring frequently.

BLANCHING ALMONDS– In a small nonmetal bowl, micro-cook 1 cup water, uncovered, on 100% power for 2-3 minutes or till boiling. Add 1/2 cup almonds to water. Micro-cook, uncovered, on 100% power for 1 1/2 minutes. Drain, rinse almonds with cold water. Slip off skins.

TOASTING COCONUT– Place flaked or shredded coconut in a 1-cup measure. Micro-cook, uncovered, on 100% power until light brown, stirring every 20 seconds. Allow 1 to 1 1/2 minutes for 1/4 cup and 1 1/2 to 2 minutes for 1/2 cup.

SOFTENING ICE CREAM– Micro-cook 1 pint solidly frozen ice cream, uncovered, on 100% power for about 15 seconds or until soft enough to serve.

PLUMPING DRIED FRUIT– In a 2-cup measure micro-cook 1 cup water, uncovered, on 100% power for 2-3 minutes or till boiling. Stir in 1/2 cup dried fruit. Let stand for 5-10 minutes.

SOFTENING BUTTER OR MARGARINE– Place unwrapped butter or margarine in a micro-safe dish. Micro-cook, uncovered, on 10% power, allowing about 25-30 seconds for 2 tablespoons or about 40 seconds for 1/4 cup butter or margarine.

SOFTENING CREAM CHEESE– Place an unwrapped 3-ounce package of cream cheese in a small micro-safe bowl. Micro-cook, uncovered on 30% power about 1 minute or until soft.

MELTING CHOCOLATE PIECES– In a glass measure micro-cook chocolate pieces, uncovered, on 100% power until melted, stirring once. Allow 1-1/2 minutes for 3 oz. or 1-1/2 to 2 minutes for a 6-ounce package.

MELTING CARAMEL– Place unwrapped caramel in a glass measure. Micro-cook, on 100% power stirring once. Allow 45 seconds to 1 minute for 14 caramels (about 1/2 cup) or 1 to 1 1/2 minutes for 28 (about a cup).

PEELING TOMATOES– In a 2-cup measure micro-cook 1 cup water, uncovered, on 100% power for 2-3 minutes or until boiling. Spear 1 tomato with a long tined fork. Submerge into hot water; hold about 12 seconds. Place tomato under cold water, slip off skin.

Cooking & Food Terms

AL DENTÉ– Describes foods, especially pasta, cooked only until soft enough to eat, but not overdone. The Italian translation is "to the teeth."

ADJUST SEASONING– To taste the dish before serving to determine the need for salt, herbs, or other seasonings.

BLACKEN– A method of cooking in which meat or fish is seasoned with a spicy mixture then fried in a hot skillet until blackened on both sides.

BLANCH– Blanching is a process in which food is briefly plunged in boiling water for a moment, then immediately transferred to ice water to stop the cooking process. Blanching tomatoes or peaches for about 20 sec. makes them easier to peel.

BRAISE– Braising involves cooking a food in a little fat to brown, usually on the stove top then covering and cooking slowly until done. This is particularly suited to less tender cuts of meat.

BROIL– To cook food directly under or over heat source, usually in the oven under the top broiling element or on the grill.

BROWN– To cook food quickly at a moderately high heat to brown the surface. May be done on the stove top or under the broiler in the oven.

BUTTERFLY– To cut a food down the center, but not quite through, leaving both halves attached, The food is then spread to resemble a butterfly.

CHUNKS– Usually bite-size pieces, about 1-inch or larger.

CLARIFIED BUTTER– Unsalted butter which has been melted and skimmed of milk solids.

CUBE– To cut into cubes, about 1/2 to 1-inch. Cube may also mean to tenderize meat with a tenderizing mallet or utensil which makes "cubes" imprints.

CURE– To preserve food, usually meat or fish, by pickling, smoking, drying, salting, or storing in a brine.

CUT IN– To incorporate solid fat into dry ingredients using a pastry blender or knives.

DASH– Less than 1/8 teaspoon.

DEEP-FAT FRY– To cook in hot fat which is deep enough to completely cover the food.

DEGLAZE– To add liquid to the pan in which meat or other food was cooked. The liquid, usually broth or wine, is heated to loosen the browned bits left in the pan, and is often used as a base for sauce or gravy.

Cooking & Food Terms

DEGREASE– To remove melted fat from the surface of liquid, usually by skimming with a spoon, refrigerating to solidify the fat, or by using a cup or pitcher designed to separate the fat from the liquid.

DEHYDRATE– To remove moisture from food by drying it slowly in the oven or in an electric or manual dehydrator.

DEVEIN– To remove the vein from the back of shrimp or to remove the interior ribs from peppers.

DICE– To cut food into cubes about 1/8 to 3/4 inch in size.

DOLLOP– A spoonful of soft food, such as mashed potatoes or whipped cream. It may also mean a dash or "splash" of soda water, water, or other liquid if referring to liquid.

DOT– To scatter bits of an ingredient (usually butter) evenly over the surface of another food.

DOUGH– A mixture of flour, liquid, and other ingredients. Dough is too thick to pour but thick enough to roll out or work with hands.

DREDGE– To coat food with a dry mixture (usually seasoned flour or crumbs), either by sprinkling, rolling, or shaking the food in a bag with the flour or other ingredients.

DRIPPINGS– The juices or liquefied fats left in a pan after cooking meat or other food.

DRIZZLE– To pour a thin mixture, such as melted butter or thin icing, over food in a very fine stream.

DUMPLING– Large or small amounts of dough usually dropped into a liquid mixture such as broth, stew, or fruit. (2) A fruit or fruit mixture encased in sweet dough and baked.

EGG WASH– Egg yolk or white mixed with a small amount of water or liquid then brushed over baked goods to give color and sheen.

EN CROUTE– Food baked in a crust.

EVAPORATED MILK– A canned, unsweetened milk is homogenized milk from which 60% of the water has been removed. Whole evaporated milk contains at least 7.9 percent butterfat, while the skim version contains 1/2 percent or less.

EXTRACT– Concentrated flavors from various foods, usually derived from distillation or evaporation. Extracts, also called essences, may be solid or liquid.

Cooking & Food Terms

FILLET– A boneless piece of meat or fish.

FLAKE– To use a fork or other utensil to break off pieces or layers of food.

FLANK STEAK– A long, fibrous cut of beef which comes from an animal's lower hindquarters. Flank steak is usually tenderized by marinating, then boiled or grilled and cut thinly across the grain.

FLOUR– To lightly sprinkle or coat with flour.

FLUTE– To press a scalloped or decorative design into the edge of a pie crust.

FOLD– To incorporate a light mixture with a heavy mixture, such as beaten egg whites into batter or custard. The lighter mixture is placed on the heavier mixture, and a spatula is used to gently cut down and through the lighter mixture of the bottom of the bowl then up again. This procedure gently turns the mixtures over on top of each other, and is repeated until the two mixtures are combined.

FRENCH FRY– To deep-fry food, such as strips of potatoes.

FRICASSEE– To cook or stew pieces of sauteed meat in a sauce, usually with vegetables. Wine is often used as a flavoring.

FRIZZLE– To fry thin slices of meat or other food until the edges curl.

FROST– To apply sugar, frosting, glaze, or icing to fruit, cake, or other food.

FRY– To cook food in a fat over moderate to high heat.

GARNISH– To decorate food or the dish on which food is served.

GLAZE– A thin, glossy coating applied to the surface of a food. A glaze may also add flavor.

GRATE– To cut food into small shreds or particles, usually with a food grater.

GRATIN DISH– A shallow baking dish or pan, usually round or oval in shape.

GREASE– To spread fat (or non-stick cooking spray) on a cooking utensil or pan to prevent food from sticking. To grease and flour means to grease the pan then dust with flour. The flour is sprinkled into the greased pan then the pan is shaken to distribute evenly before inverting and discarding the excess.

GRILL– To cook on a rack directly over hot coals or other heat source.

Cooking & Food Terms

GRIND– To reduce food to small particles, as in ground coffee, ground beef, or ground spices. A variety of instruments may be used, including mortar and pestle, meat grinder, pepper mills, and food processor.

HALF AND HALF– A mixture of half cream, half milk. The fat content is between 10 and 12 percent.

INFUSE– To immerse tea, herbs, or other flavoring ingredients in a hot liquid in order to extract flavor.

JELL– To congeal, often with the addition of gelatin.

JIGGER– A liquid measure equal to 1-1/2 fluid ounces.

JULIENNE– To cut food into thin, matchstick strips. Julienne strips are usually about 1/8 inch thick, but the length varies.

KNEAD– A technique used to mix and work dough, usually using the hands. Dough is pressed with the heels of the hands, while stretching it out, then folded over itself.

LARD– Rendered and clarified pork fat. As a verb, to lard is to insert strips of fat into uncooked lean meat (such as venison) to tenderize and add flavor.

LEAVENER– An ingredient or agent used to lighten the texture and increase volume in baked goods. Baking powder, baking soda, and yeast are common leaveners.

LIQUEUR– Sweet alcoholic drink usually served after a meal. Liqueurs are usually flavored with aromatic ingredients such as nuts, fruits, flowers, or spices, and are frequently used in baked desserts and dessert sauces.

MARINATE– To let food soak in a seasoned liquid in order to flavor and tenderize.

MASH– To crush a food until smooth and evenly textured.

MEDALLION– A small, round cut of meat, usually pork, veal, or beef.

MELT– Heating a food (such as shortening, butter, or chocolate) until it becomes liquid.

MINCE– To chop food into small pieces, usually 1/8 inch or less.

MIX– To blend ingredients.

MOLD– To form a food into a shape by hand, or by placing or pouring into a decorative container (or mold) then refrigerating or cooking until firm enough to hold its shape.

MOUSSE– A sweet or savory dish, made with egg whites or whipped cream to give the light, airy texture.

Cooking & Food Terms

MULL– To flavor a beverage, such as cider or wine, by heating it with spices or other flavorings.

PARBOIL– To boil a food briefly, until partially done. A food might be parboiled before adding it to faster-cooking ingredients to insure all ingredients are evenly cooked.

PARE– To cut the skin from a food, usually with a short knife called a paring knife.

PASTEURIZE– To kill bacteria by heating liquids to moderately high temperatures only briefly. French scientist Louis Pasteur discovered the solution while he was researching the cause of beer and wine spoilage.

PASTRY BAG– A cone-shaped bag with openings at both ends. Food is placed into the large opening then squeezed out the small opening which may be fitted with a decorator tip. It has a variety of uses, including decorating cakes and cookies, forming pastries, or piping decorative edging. Bags may be made of cloth, plastic, or other materials.

PASTRY BLENDER– A kitchen utensil with several u-shaped wires attached to a handle. It's used to cut solid fat (like shortening or butter) into flour and other dry ingredients in order to evenly distribute the fat particles.

PASTRY BRUSH– A brush used to apply glaze or egg wash to breads and other baked goods either before or after baking.

PASTRY WHEEL– A utensil with a cutting wheel attached to a handle. It's used to mark and cut rolled-out dough, and may have a plain or decorative edge.

PIPE– To squeeze icing or other soft food through a pastry bag to make a design or decorative edible edging.

PIQUANT– A term which generally means tangy flavor.

PIT– To remove the seed or stone of a fruit or berry.

POACH– To cook in liquid at or just below the boiling point. For eggs, meat, or fish, the liquid is usually water or a seasoned stock; fruit is generally poached in a sugar syrup.

PREHEAT– To allow the oven or pan to get to a specified temperature before adding the food to be cooked.

PRESERVE– To prepare foods for long storage. Some ways to preserve foods are drying, freezing, canning, curing, pickling, and smoking.

PRICK– To make small holes in the surface of a food, usually using the tines of a fork. Pie crust is usually pricked.

Cooking & Food Terms

PULVERIZE– To reduce to a powder or dust by pounding, crushing or grinding.

PUREE– To blend, process, sieve, or mash a food until it's very smooth and has the consistency of baby food.

REDUCE– To boil a liquid until a portion of it has evaporated. Reducing intensifies the flavor and results in a thicker liquid.

RENDER– To extract the fat from meat by cooking over low heat. Rendered fat is strained of meat particles after cooking.

ROAST– To cook food in an open pan in the oven, with no added liquid.

ROLLING BOIL– A very fast boil that doesn't slow when stirred.

SAUTÉ– To cook quickly in a pan on top of the stove until the food is browned.

SCORE– To cut shallow slashes unto ham or other food, to allow excess fat to drain, or to help tenderize.

SEAR– To brown meat quickly over high heat. Meat may be seared under a broiler or in a skillet on top of the stove.

SHRED– To cut food into narrow strips. A grater or food processor may be used to shred.

SIFT– To pass dry ingredients through a mesh sifter. Incorporates air, which makes food lighter.

SIMMER– To cook liquid at about 185° or just below boil. Tiny bubbles just beginning to break the surface.

SKIM– To remove a substance from the surface of a liquid.

SLIVER– To cut a food into thin strips or pieces.

STEEP– To soak, in order to extract flavor or soften.

STRAIN– To pour liquid through a strainer or colander to remove solid particles.

THICKEN– To make liquid more thick by reducing or adding a roux, starch, or eggs.

THIN– To dilute a mixture by adding more liquid.

TRUSS– To hold food together so it will retain its shape. Poultry and some roasts are often tied with twine or held together with skewers.

WATERBATH– To place a container of food in a large pan of warm water, which surrounds the food with heat.

WHIP– To beat ingredients with a whisk, or other utensil, which incorporates air into a mixture and changes the texture.

Ingredient Substitutions

INGREDIENT	AMOUNT	SUBSTITUTE
Allspice	1 tsp.	• 1/2 tsp. cinnamon and 1/2 tsp. ground cloves
Apple Pie Spice	1 tsp.	• 1/2 tsp. cinnamon, 1/4 tsp. nutmeg, and 1/8 tsp. cardamom
Arrowroot	1 1/2 tsp.	• 1 tsp flour • 1 1/2 tsp. cornstarch
Baking Powder	1 tsp.	• 1/3 tsp. baking soda and 1/2 tsp. cream of tartar • 1/4 tsp. baking soda and 1/2 cup sour milk or buttermilk (Decrease liquid called for in recipe by 1/2 cup.)
Bay Leaf	1 whole	• 1/8 to 1/4 tsp., crushed
Bread	1 slice dry 1 slice soft	• 1/3 cup dry bread crumbs • 3/4 cup bread crumbs
Broth, Beef or Chicken	1 cup	• 1 bouillon cube dissolved in 1 cup boiling water • 1 envelope powdered broth base dissolved in 1 cup boiling water • 1 1/2 tsp. powdered broth base dissolved in 1 cup boiling water
Butter	1 cup	• 7/8 to 1 cup hydrogenated fat and 1/2 tsp. salt • 7/8 cup lard plus 1/2 tsp. salt • 1 cup margarine
Buttermilk (sour milk)	1 cup	• 1 cup plain yogurt • 1 cup whole or skim milk plus 1 Tbsp. lemon juice or white vinegar • 1 cup milk plus 1 3/4 tsp. cream of tartar
Chili Sauce	1 cup	• 1 cup catsup, 1/4 tsp. cinnamon, dashes of ground cloves and allspice

Ingredient Substitutions

INGREDIENT	AMOUNT	SUBSTITUTE
Chives, Finely Chopped	2 tsp.	• 2 tsp. green onion tops finely chopped
Chocolate, Chips Semisweet	1 oz.	• 1 oz. sweet cooking chocolate
Chocolate, Semisweet	1 2/3 oz. 6 oz. pkg.	• 1 oz. unsweetened chocolate plus 4 tsp. sugar • 1 cup
Chocolate, Unsweetened	1 oz. sq.	• 3 Tbsp. cocoa plus 1 Tbsp. fat
Cocoa	1/4 cup or 4 Tbsp.	• 1 oz. sq. unsweetened chocolate (decrease fat called for in recipe by 1/2 Tbsp.)
Coconut Cream	1 cup	• 1 cup whipping cream
Coconut Milk	1 cup	• 1 cup whole or 2% milk
Corn	1 doz. ears	• 2 1/2 cups cooked
Cornmeal, Self-rising	1 cup	• 7/8 cup plain, 1 1/2 Tbsp. baking powder, and 1/2 tsp. salt
Corn Syrup, Dark	1 cup	• 3/4 cup light corn syrup and 1/4 cup light molasses
Cornstarch (for thickening)	1 Tbsp.	• 2 Tbsp. all purpose flour • 2 Tbsp. granular tapioca
Cracker Crumbs	3/4 cup	• 1 cup dry bread crumbs
Cream, Heavy (36% to 40% fat)	1 cup	• 3/4 cup milk and 1/3 cup butter or margarine (for use in cooking or baking)

Ingredient Substitutions

INGREDIENT	AMOUNT	SUBSTITUTE
Cream, Light (18% to 20% fat)	1 cup	• 3/4 cup milk and 3 Tbsp. butter or margarine (for use in cooking or baking) • 1 cup evaporated milk, undiluted
Cream, Whipped	2 tsp.	• Chill a 13 oz-can of evaporated milk until ice crystals form. Add 1 tsp. lemon juice. Whip until stiff
Dates	1 lb.	• 2 1/2 cups pitted
Dill Plant, Fresh or Dried	3 heads	• 1 Tbsp. dill seed
Egg, Whole, Uncooked	1 large (3 Tbsp.)	• 3 Tbsp. and 1 tsp. thawed frozen egg • 2 1/2 Tbsp. sifted, dry whole egg powder and 2 1/2 Tbsp. lukewarm water • 2 yolks 1 Tbsp. water (in cookies) • 2 yolks (in custard, cream fillings, and similar mixture) • 2 whites as a thickening agent
Eggs, Uncooked	1 cup = ▸	• 5 large • 6 medium
Egg White	1 large (2 Tbsp.) 1 cup = ▸	• 2 Tbsp. sifted, dry egg white powder, and 2 Tbsp. lukewarm water • 8 large egg whites
Egg Yolk (1 1/2 Tbsp.)	1 yolk 1 cup = ▸	• 3 1/2 Tbsp. thawed frozen egg yolk • 2 Tbsp. sifted, dry egg yolk • 12 large egg yolks
Fines Herbes	1/3 cup	• 3 Tbsp. parsley flakes, 2 tsp. dried chervil, 2 tsp. dried chives, 1 tsp. dried tarragon

Ingredient Substitutions

INGREDIENT	AMOUNT	SUBSTITUTE
Flour, All-purpose (for thickening)	1 Tbsp.	• 1 1/2 tsp. cornstarch, arrowroot starch, potato starch, or rice starch • 1 tsp. waxy rice flour • 1 1/2 Tbsp. whole wheat flour • 1 tsp. quick-cooking tapioca
Flour, All-purpose	1 cup sifted	• 1 cup and 2 Tbsp. cake flour • 1 cup rolled oats, crushed
	1 lb.	• 4 cups sifted • 3 1/3 cups unsifted
Flour, Cake	1 lb.	• 4 3/4 cups
	1 cup sifted	• 1 cup minus 2 Tbsp. sifted all-purpose flour
Flour, Self-rising	1 cup	• 1 cup minus 2 tsp. all-purpose flour, 1 1/2 tsp. baking powder, and 1/2 tsp. salt

NOTE: Substitutes for white flours added to most baked goods will result in a reduced volume and a heavier product. Substitute no more than 1/4 of white flour in a cake to ensure success. In other recipes, you can substitute whole wheat flour for 1/4 to 1/2 white flour.

Garlic	1 clove	• 1/8 tsp. garlic powder
Gelatin, Flavored	3 oz.	• 1 Tbsp. plain gelatin and 2 cups of fruit juice
Honey	1 cup	• 1 1/4 cup sugar and 1/4 cup water
Ketchup	1 cup	• 1 cup tomato sauce, 1/4 cup brown sugar, and 2 Tbsp. vinegar (for use in cooking)
Lemon Juice	1 tsp.	• 1/2 tsp. vinegar
Lemon Peel, Dried	1 tsp.	• 1 to 2 tsp. grated fresh lemon peel • 1/2 tsp. lemon extract

Ingredient Substitutions

INGREDIENT	AMOUNT	SUBSTITUTE
Marshmallows, Miniature	1 cup	• 8-10 regular
Mayonnaise	1 cup	• 1/2 cup yogurt and 1/2 cup mayonnaise • 1 cup of sour cream
Milk, Buttermilk	1 cup	• 1 cup sweet milk and 1 3/4 tsp. cream of tartar
Milk, Skim	1 cup	• 1/2 cup evaporated milk and 1/2 cup water
Milk, Sweetened	1 can (about 1 1/3 cups)	• Heat the following ingredients until sugar and butter are dissolved: 1/3 cup plus 2 tsp. evaporated milk, 1 cup sugar, and 3 Tbsp. butter or margarine
Milk, Whole	1 cup	• 1 cup reconstituted non-fat dry milk (Add 2 Tbsp. butter or margarine, if desired.) • 1/2 cup evaporated milk and 1/2 cup water
Mustard, Dry	1 tsp.	• 1 Tbsp. prepared mustard
Onion, Fresh	1 small	• Rehydrate 1 Tbsp. instant minced onion
Onion, Powdered	1 Tbsp.	• 1 medium onion • 4 Tbsp. fresh chopped
Onion	1 lb.	• 3 large onions • 2 to 2 1/2 cups chopped
Orange Peel, Dried	1 Tbsp.	• 2 to 3 Tbsp. grated orange peel
Parsley, Dried	1 tsp.	• 3 tsp. fresh parsley, chopped

Ingredient Substitutions

INGREDIENT	AMOUNT	SUBSTITUTE
Pumpkin Pie Spice	1 tsp.	• 1/2 tsp. cinnamon, 1/4 tsp. ginger, 1/8 tsp. allspice, and 1/8 tsp. nutmeg
Shortening, Melted	1 cup	• 1 cup cooking oil (Substitute only if recipe calls for melted shortening)
Shortening, Solid (used in baking)	1 cup	• 1 1/8 cups butter (Decrease salt called for in recipe by 1/2 tsp.)
Sour Cream, Cultured	1 cup	• 1 cup plain yogurt • 3/4 cup milk, 3/4 tsp. lemon juice, and 1/3 cup butter or margarine
Sugar, Brown	1 cup firmly packed	• 1 cup granulated sugar
	1 lb. = ▸	• 2 1/4 cups firmly packed
Sugar, Granulated	1 lb. = ▸	• 2 1/4 cups
Sugar, Powdered	1 lb. = ▸	• 2 3/4 cups
Sugar, Granulated	1 tsp.	• 1/8 tsp. noncaloric sweetener solution or follow manufacturer's directions
Sugar, Granulated	1 cup	• 1 1/2 cups corn syrup (Decrease liquid called for in recipe by 1/4 cup.) • 1 cup of powdered sugar • 1 cup, brown sugar, firmly packed • 3/4 cup honey (Decrease liquid called for in recipe by 1/4 cup; for each cup of honey in baked goods, add 1/2 tsp. soda.)
Tomato Juice	1 cup	• 1 cup tomato sauce and 1/2 cup water
Yogurt, Plain	1 cup	• 1 cup of buttermilk • 1 cup of sour cream

Yields & Equivalents

FOOD	YOUR RECIPE STATES	YOU WILL NEED
Apples	▸ 1 cup sliced or chopped ▸ 1 lb.	◂ 1 medium (6 oz.) ◂ 3 medium
Apricots, Dried Halves	1 cup	5 oz.
Asparagus	16 to 20 stalks	1 lb.
Bacon	1/2 cup crumbled	8 slices, crisply cooked
Bananas	▸ 1 cup sliced ▸ 1 cup mashed	◂ 1 medium or 2 small ◂ 2 medium
Beans	5 to 6 cups cooked	1 lb. dried (2 1/4 cups)
Beans, Green or Wax	3 cups 1-inch pieces	1 lb.
Bread, White	▸ 12 slices (1/2 inch) ▸ 1 cup soft ▸ 1 cup dry	◂ 1-lb loaf ◂ 1 1/2 slices ◂ 4 to 5 slices, oven-dried
Broccoli	2 cups flowerets, 1-inch pieces or chopped	6 oz.
Butter	1/2 cup	1 stick
Cabbage, Green Slaw (bag)	▸ 1 medium head ▸ 4 cups shredded	◂ 1 1/2 lb. ◂ 1 lb.
Carrots	▸ 1 medium ▸ 1 cup shredded ▸ 1 cup 1/4-inch slices	◂ 7 inches ◂ 1 1/2 medium ◂ 2 medium
Cauliflower	▸ 1 medium head ▸ 3 cups flowerets	◂ 2 lb. (with leaves) ◂ 1 lb.
Celery	▸ 1 medium bunch ▸ 1 cup thinly sliced or chopped	◂ 2 lb. (11 inches) ◂ 2 medium stalks

Yields & Equivalents

FOOD	YOUR RECIPE STATES	YOU WILL NEED
Cheese, Hard Cottage Cream	▸ 1 cup ▸ 2 cups ▸ 1 cup	◂ 4 oz. ◂ 16 oz. ◂ 8 oz.
Corn, Sweet	▸ 1 medium ear ▸ 1 cup kernels	◂ 8 oz. ◂ 2 medium ears
Cream, Sour Whipping (heavy)	▸ 1 cup ▸ 1 cup (2 cups whipped)	◂ 8 oz. ◂ 1/2 pt.
Crumbs, Finely Crushed Chocolate Wafer Cookie Graham Cracker Saltine Cracker Vanilla Wafer	▸ 1 1/2 cups ▸ 1 1/2 cups ▸ 1 cup ▸ 1 1/2 cups	◂ 27 cookies ◂ 21 squares ◂ 29 squares ◂ 38 cookies
Eggs, Large Whole	▸ 1 cup ▸ 1 egg	◂ 4 large ◂ 1/4 cup fat free egg product
Flour	3 1/2 cups	1 lb.
Garlic	1/2 tsp. finely chopped	1 medium clove
Lemons or Limes	▸ 1 1/2 to 3 tsp. grated peel ▸ 2 to 3 Tbsp. juice	◂ 1 medium ◂ 1 medium
Meat, Cooked Beef, Pork and Poultry	1 cup chopped or bite-size pieces	6 oz.
Mushrooms, Fresh	▸ 6 cups sliced ▸ 2 1/2 cups chopped	◂ 1 lb. ◂ 8 oz.
Canned	4-oz. can sliced, drained	◂ 2/3 cup fresh, sliced and cooked (5 oz. uncooked)

Yields & Equivalents

FOOD	YOUR RECIPE STATES	YOU WILL NEED
Nuts, (without shells) Chopped, Sliced or Slivered	▸ 1 cup	◂ 4 oz.
Whole or Halves	▸ 3 to 4 cups	◂ 1 lb.
Olives, Pimiento-stuffed Ripe, Pitted	▸ 1 cup sliced ▸ 1 cup sliced	◂ 24 large or 36 small ◂ 32 medium
Oranges	▸ 1 Tbsp. grated peel ▸ 1/3 to 1/2 cup juice	◂ 1 medium ◂ 1 medium
Pasta, Macaroni Noodles, egg Spaghetti	▸ 4 cups cooked ▸ 4 cups cooked ▸ 4 cups cooked	◂ 2 cups uncooked (6-7 oz.) ◂ 4 to 5 cups uncooked (7 oz.) ◂ 7 to 8 oz. uncooked
Peppers, Bell	▸ 1/2 cup chopped ▸ 1 cup chopped ▸ 1 1/2 cups chopped	◂ 1 small ◂ 1 medium ◂ 1 large
Rice, Brown Parboiled (converted) Precooked White Instant Regular Long Grain Wild	▸ 4 cups cooked ▸ 3 to 4 cups cooked ▸ 2 cups cooked ▸ 3 cups cooked ▸ 3 cups cooked	◂ 1 cup uncooked ◂ 1 cup uncooked ◂ 1 cup uncooked ◂ 1 cup uncooked ◂ 1 cup uncooked
Shrimp (uncooked, with shells) Jumbo Large Medium Small	▸ 1 lb. ▸ 1 lb. ▸ 1 lb. ▸ 1 lb.	◂ 21 to 25 count ◂ 31 to 35 count ◂ 41 to 45 count ◂ 51 to 60 count
Cooked (without shells)	▸ 1 lb.	◂ 1 1/3 lb. uncooked (with shells)

Yields & Equivalents

TEASPOONS	TEASPOONS	CUPS	FLUID OZ.	MILLILITERS	OTHER
1/4 teaspoon				1 ml.	
1/2 teaspoon				2 ml.	
3/4 teaspoon	1/4 tablespoon			4 ml.	
1 teaspoon	1/3 tablespoon			5 ml.	
3 teaspoons	1 tablespoon	1/16 cup	1/2 oz.	15 ml.	
6 teaspoons	2 tablespoons	1/8 cup	1 oz.	30 ml.	
			1 1/2 oz.	44 ml.	1 jigger
12 teaspoons	4 tablespoons	1/4 cup	2 oz.	60 ml.	
16 teaspoons	5 1/3 tablespoons	1/3 cup	2 1/2 oz.	75 ml.	
18 teaspoons	6 tablespoons	3/8 cup	3 oz.	90 ml.	
24 teaspoons	8 tablespoons	1/2 cup	4 oz.	125 ml.	1/4 pint
32 teaspoons	10 2/3 tablespoons	2/3 cup	5 oz.	150 ml.	
36 teaspoons	12 tablespoons	3/4 cup	6 oz.	175 ml.	
48 teaspoons	16 tablespoons	1 cup	8 oz.	237 ml.	1/2 pint
		1 1/2 cups	12 oz.	355 ml.	
		2 cups	16 oz.	473 ml.	1 pint
		3 cups	24 oz.	710 ml.	1 1/2 pints
			25.6 oz.	757 ml.	1 fifth
		4 cups	32 oz.	946 ml.	1 quart or 1 liter
		8 cups	64 oz.		2 quarts
		16 cups	128 oz.		1 gallon

Dash or Pinch– Less than 1/8 tsp.

Firmly Packed– Tightly pressed ingredients in measuring cup.

Lightly Packed– Lightly pressed ingredients in measuring cup.

Even / Level– Precise measure. Discard any ingredients that rise above the rim of the measuring cup.

Rounded– Allow ingredients to pile above the rim measuring cup into a nice round shape.

Heaping– Pile as much of the ingredient on top of the measure as it can hold.

Sifted– Sift before measuring to ensure ingredient is not compacted.

General Oven Chart

Very Slow Oven	250 to 300° F.
Slow Oven	300 to 325° F.
Moderate Oven	325 to 375° F.
Medium Hot Oven	375 to 400° F.
Hot Oven	400 to 450° F.
Very Hot Oven	450 to 500° F

BREADS

Baking Powder Biscuits	400° F.	12 - 15 min.
Muffins	400° - 425° F.	25 - 35 min.
Quick Breads	350° - 375° F.	25 - 35 min.
Yeast Breads	375° - 400° F.	45 - 60 min.
Yeast Rolls	400° F.	15 - 20 min.

CAKES

Butter Loaf Cakes	350° F.	45 - 60 min.
Butter Layer Cakes	350° - 375° F.	25 - 35 min.
Cup Cakes	375° F.	20 - 23 min.
Chiffon Cakes	325° F.	60 min.
Sponge Cakes	325° F.	60 min.
Angel Food Cakes	325° F.	60 min.

COOKIES

Bar Cookies	350° F.	25 - 30 min.
Drop Cookies	350° - 375° F.	18 - 25 min.
Rolled Refrigerator Cookies	350° - 400° F.	8 - 12 min.

PASTRY

Meringue	350° F.	12 - 20 min.
Pie Shells	450° F.	12 - 15 min.
Filled Pies	450° F.	
	lower to 350° F.	8 - 12 min.

NOTES: These are just general temperatures and times, always use what is specified in the recipe.

Modern oven thermostats are adjustable, so it is necessary to periodically check the ACTUAL oven temperature with an accurate thermometer designed for the purpose and adjust the dial, or have your serviceman perform this service at least once a year.

Always follow HIGH ALTITUDE directions, temperature settings and times when appropriate to your locale.

Meats
Seasonings & Marinades

FLAVORING CHART

MEAT	SEASONINGS			
Beef	rosemary sage garlic dill	mushrooms dry mustard shallots paprika	chili peppers peppercorns berries tomatoes	beer red wine balsamic vinegar
Chicken or Turkey	lemon ginger tarragon sage	thyme oregano dill peppers	garlic apple cider dry mustard fruit juices	paprika red wine white wine
Fish	cilantro bay leaf basil fennel	lemon lime dill saffron	black pepper garlic sweet peppers tarragon	rosemary herbed vinegar
Lamb	garlic curry mint lemon	rosemary thyme sage ginger	saffron mustard seed	
Pork	apples garlic ginger lemon	cloves rosemary orange zest lemon zest	coriander unsweetened preserves dried fruits	Madeira or port wine
Veal	ginger oregano mustard marjoram	shallots mushrooms orange lemon	Marsala wine garlic thyme	
Veg.	garlic lemon dill vinegar	nuts parsley mint rosemary	basil allspice sweet peppers pepper flakes	marjoram chervil chives nutmeg

TIP: For added flavor, blend garlic and herbs (fresh or dried) into a dish ahead of time. At the last minute of cooking time, toss in. This gives an extra dimension in taste.

Meats
Doneness Chart

DESCRIPTION	DEGREES FAHRENHEIT
Ground Meat & Mixtures	
Turkey, Chicken	165° F.
Veal, Beef, Lamb, Pork	160° F.
Fresh Beef	
Medium Rare	145° F.
Medium	160° F.
Well Done	170° F.
Fresh Veal	
Medium Rare	145° F.
Medium	160° F.
Well Done	170° F.
Fresh Lamb	
Medium Rare	145° F.
Medium	160° F.
Well Done	170° F.
Pork	
Well Done	170° F.
Poultry	
Chicken, Whole	180° F.
Turkey, Whole	180° F.
Poultry Breasts, Roasted	170° F.
Poultry Thighs, Wings	180° F.
Duck & Goose	180° F.
Seafood	
Fin Fish	Cook until opaque and flakes easily.
Shrimp, Lobster, Crab	Shell should turn red. Flesh pearly opaque.
Scallops	Flesh should turn milky white or opaque and firm.
Clams, Mussels, Oysters	Cook until shells open. Discard any unopened.

Candy Making Chart

Important tips to remember when making candy:

1. Dissolve sugar completely to keep large crystals from forming; wash down the sides of the saucepan by placing a cover over the saucepan for about 2-3 minutes.

2. Heavy, flat bottom saucepans will prevent candies from scorching.

3. A candy thermometer is essential for proper temperature.

4. Cool fudges to lukewarm before beating or shaping.

5. Butter, not margarine, should be used in most candy recipes to ensure the best textures and results.

Thread	begins at 230°	The syrup will make a 2" thread when dropped from a spoon.
Soft Ball	begins at 234°	A small amount of syrup dropped into chilled water forms a ball, but flattens when picked up with fingers.
Firm Ball	begins at 244°	The ball will hold its shape and flatten only when pressed.
Hard Ball	begins at 250°	The ball is more rigid but still pliable.
Soft Crack	begins at 270°	When a small amount of syrup is dropped into chilled water it will separate into threads which will bend when picked up.
Hard Crack	begins at 300°	The syrup separates into threads that are hard and brittle.
Caramelized	Sugar 310° to 338°	Between these temperatures the syrup will turn dark golden, but will turn black at 350°.

Herbs & Spices

ALLSPICE– Usually used in ground form, allspice has a flavor like a combination of cinnamon, nutmeg, and cloves. Allspice is used in both savory and sweet dishes.

ANISE SEED– Related to parsley, this spice has a mildly sweet licorice flavor.

BASIL– Most people are accustomed to using fresh basil in their favorite Italian dishes, but this licorice-like herb is equally at home in Thai coconut curry or a Provencal pistou. Dried basil tastes completely different from fresh, so if you want to add a shot of basil flavor try blending basil with olive oil and storing cubes in the freezer.

BAY LEAF– A pungent flavor. Available as whole leaf. Good in vegetable and fish soups, tomato sauces and juice. Remove before serving.

CARAWAY– Their slightly anise flavor works particularly well with rye breads as well with the kind of sweet and sour dishes favored in Central Europe such as pork and apples or braised red cabbage.

CARDAMOM– Whole cardamom pods can appear in pilaf rice, curries, or Scandinavian baked goods. Ground cardamom loses its flavor.

CAYENNE PEPPER– A touch of spicy cayenne can add a lot of heat to a dish without radically changing the flavor It is a mixture of ground chili peppers and can be used in a wide variety of cuisines.

CELERY SEED– The wild celery plant these seeds are from are on more and more menus emphasizing regional and local cuisine. The seeds add their pungent flavor to anything from cocktails to coleslaw and can be used whole or ground.

CHIVES– Leaves are used in many ways. May be used in salads, cream cheese, sandwiches, omelets, soups, and fish dishes.

CILANTRO– This herb is truly a love it or hate it proposition. Stems are quite sweet and can be added raw along with the leaves while the roots are prized by Thai chefs for curry pastes.

CINNAMON– Cinnamon adds sweetness and heat to sweet and savory dishes alike. Cinnamon sticks are often added whole to coffee, stews, rice, curries, or tangines and removed before serving. It is a staple in baked goods–a sprinkle makes even a simple bowl of oatmeal smell and taste great.

CLOVE– Often paired with cinnamon and nutmeg, cloves are dried flower buds that are sold both ground and whole. They have a warm, sweet flavor that works great with sweet and savory, like clove studded ham. For a more potent flavor grind them yourself.

CUMIN– Can be experienced in all kinds of dishes from Mexico, India and the Middle East. The toasted seeds can be used whole in dishes and eaten as is, or be ground right before use. Pre-ground cumin loses potency quickly, but can be helped by toasting first in a dry skillet over medium-low heat.

Herbs & Spices

DILL– The feathery leaves of the dill plant add light anise flavor to seafood, soups, salads, and lots of other dishes. Dill is almost always added at the very last minute. Keep fresh in the refrigerator by storing it in a glass of water with a plastic bag placed over the top.

GINGER– There are many ways to use this peppery root from fresh to dried and ground to pickled or crystallized. Each of these preparations adds unique flavors and textures to everything from stir-fries to roasted meats to classic ginger snaps.

MINT– Commonly associated with sweet treats, mint lends its cooling, peppery bite to plenty of savory dishes, particularly from the Middle East and North Africa. Perfect for summer-fresh salads or to liven up a sauce, leftover fresh mint can also be used to brew a fragrant tea which is equally tasty served hot or cold.

MUSTARD– Mustard is great to have around to add heat and a piquant flavor in sauces, dressings, marinades, and entrees. Whole mustard seeds are often part of the pickling spices, but are also a key part of many Indian curries where they are toasted in oil first until they pop.

NUTMEG– An aromatic spice with a sweet and spicy flavor. Nutmeg adds warmth and depth to foods but doesn't overpower other ingredients.

OREGANO– A pungent herb primarily found in Mediterranean and Mexican cuisines, it is one of the few herbs that survives the drying process relatively unscathed. Use dried oregano for longer stewing or dry rubs, but make sure to use half as much dry as you would fresh since the flavor is so intense. Oregano can also be used as a substitute for its close cousin marjoram.

PAPRIKA– Paprika has too often been relegated to the role of garnish, mostly because of its beautiful rich color. There are all sorts of paprika that can add flavors from mild to hot.

PARSLEY– Formerly regulated to the role of garnish, fresh parsley is coming into its own for its fresh flavor and great health benefits, but dried parsley lacks both flavor and color.

PEPPERCORN– Along with salt, black pepper is half of a team that is so fundamental to cooking that they get called upon nearly every time you need to spice up a dish. There are all sorts of peppercorns that each offer their own flavors and degrees of heat.

RED PEPPER– Dried red chili pepper sold either ground or in flakes, red pepper works well either added early to dishes that are going to cook for a while or simply shaken on near the very end. Because they vary greatly in terms of heat, taste your red pepper to see just how hot it is.

ROSEMARY– Can be used fresh or dried for long cooking in soups, meats, stews and more. Use sparingly at first and more if needed.

Herbs & Spices

SAGE– Used fresh. May be used in poultry and meat stuffings; in sausage and practically all meat combinations; in cheese and vegetable combinations, or curry.

TARRAGON– Experimenting with this anise-like herb in classic French favorites such as bearnaise sauce, creamy tarragon chicken, or fresh vinaigrette can help you learn how to use tarragon to lift flavors without overpowering a dish.

THYME– One of the most popular herbs in American and European cooking, thyme can be paired with nearly any kind of meat, poultry, fish, or vegetable. To use fresh thyme, peel off as many of the leaves as you can from the woody stem by running your fingers along the stem.

VANILLA– An aromatic spice with a warm flavor, vanilla is the seed pod of an orchid. It's available dried or as an extract.

HERB AND SPICE TIPS

In contrast to herbs, spices are nearly always dried and are mostly ground before using. Pre-ground spices lose their potency quickly, so they should be stored in airtight containers in a cool, dark place and be replaced around every six months. Whole spices retain their flavor longer (for up to five years) and can be used as is or quickly ground with mortar and pestle or an inexpensive coffee grinder (reserve one for spices to avoid coffee flavor).

To get the best flavor from your spices, "toast" them in a dry skillet over low heat, stirring frequently, until they start to release their aromas. Even ground spices can perk up a bit after a quick toast in a skillet, but ones that are too old and faded are generally beyond repair.

FRESH SEASONINGS

- In recipes, cut salt in half and add more fresh herbs and spices.
- When doubling a recipe, herbs and spices should only be increased by one and a half times. Taste, and then add some if necessary.
- Add sage, bay leaf and garlic at the beginning of the cooking process as they have a strong flavor. Herbs with more subtle aroma such as basil, parsley, fennel are best when added at the end of the cooking process to preserve their flavor.
- Delicate aromas can be lost due to overcooking.
- Cut or chop fresh herbs to expose more surface area. This will release more flavor.
- Here's a chart to convert dried herbs to fresh

1 tsp. dried herbs	=	1 Tbsp. fresh herbs
1/8 tsp. garlic powder	=	1 medium clove of garlic
1 tsp. onion powder	=	1 medium onion, finely chopped
1 tsp. ground ginger	=	1 tsp. grated fresh ginger

Cooking Vegetables

- Times on chart are for fresh, one pound vegetables.
- The cooking times are in minutes.
- NR = Not recommended.
- Steaming times begin when the water boils and creates steam.
- Vegetables are done when they are tender, but still crisp. (They should not be mushy.)

VEGETABLES	STEAM	MICRO.	BLANCH	BOIL	OTHER
Artichoke, whole	30-60	4-5 each	NR	25-40	NR
Artichoke, hearts	10-15	6-7	8-12	10-15	Stir-fry 10
Asparagus	8-10	4-6	2-3	5-12	Stir-fry pieces 5
Beans, green	5-15	6-12	4-5	10-20	Stir-fry 3-4
Beans, lima	10-20	8-12	5-10	20-30	NR
Beets	40-60	14-18	NR	30-60	Bake 60
Broccoli, spears	8-15	6-7	3-4	5-10	Blanch; Bake
Broccoli flowerets	5-6	4-5	2-3	4-5	Stir-fry 3-4
Brussels sprouts	6-12	7-8	4-5	5-10	Halve; Stir-fry 3-4
Cabbage, wedges	6-9	10-12	NR	10-15	
Carrots, whole	10-15	8-10	4-5	15-20	Bake 30-40
Carrots, sliced	4-5	4-7	3-4	5-10	Stir-fry 3-4
Cauliflower, whole	15-20	6-7	4-5	10-15	Blanch; Bake 20
Cauliflower, flowerets	6-10	3-5	3-4	5-8	Stir-fry 3-4
Corn, on cob	6-10	3-4	3-4	4-7	Soak 10; bake 375°
Corn, cut	4-6	2 per cup	2 12-4	3-4	Stir-fry 3-4
Eggplant, whole	15-30	7-10	10-15	10-15	Bake 30 at 400°
Eggplant, diced	5-6	5-6	3-4	5-10	Bake 10-15 425°
Greens, Collard, turnip	NR	18-20	8-15	30-60	Stir-fry 4-6
Greens, kale/beet	4-6	8-10	4-5	5-8	Stir-fry 2-3
Mushrooms	4-5	3-4	NR	3-4 /broth	Stir-fry or broil 4-5
Onions, whole	20-25	6-10	NR	20-30	Bake 60 at 325°
Onions, pearl	15-20	5-7	2-3	10-20	Braise 15-25
Parsnips	8-10	4-6	3-4	5-10	Bake 30 at 325°
Peas	3-5	5-7	1-2	8-12	Stir-fry 2-3
Peppers, bell	2-4	2-4	2-3	4-5	Stir-fry 2-3
Potatoes, whole	12-30	6-8	NR	20-30	Bake 40-60 at 400°
Potatoes, cut	10-12	8-10	NR	15-20	Bake 25-30 at 400°
Spinach	5-6	3-4	2-3	2-5	Stir-fry 2-3
Squash, sliced	5-10	3-6	2-3	5-10	NR
Squash, halves	15-40	6-10	NR	5-10	Bake 40-60 at 375°
Tomatoes	2-3	3-4	1-2	NR	Bake halves 8-15
Turnips, cubed	12-15	6-8	2-3	5-8	Stir-fry 2-3
Zucchini	5-10	3-6	2-3	5-10	Broil halves 5

Counting Calories

CANDIES, SNACKS & NUTS

Almonds	12 to 15	93
Cashews	6 to 8	88
Chocolate Bar (nut)	2 ounce bar	340
Coconut (shredded)	1 cup	344
English Toffee	1 piece	25
Fudge	1 ounce	115
Mints	5 very small	50
Peanuts (salted)	1 ounce	190
Peanuts (roasted)	1 cup	800
Pecans	6	104
Popcorn (plain)	1 cup	54
Potato Chips	10 medium chips	115
Pretzels	10 small sticks	35
Walnuts	8 to 10	100

DAIRY PRODUCTS

American Cheese	1 cube $1\frac{1}{8}$ inch	100
Butter, margarine	1 level Tbsp.	100
Cheese (blue, cheddar, cream, Swiss)	1 ounce	105
Cottage Cheese (uncreamed)	1 ounce	25
Cream(light)	1 Tbsp.	30
Egg White	1	15
Egg Yolk	1	61
Eggs (boiled or poached)	2	160
Eggs (scrambled)	2	220
Eggs (fried)	1 medium	110
Yogurt (flavored)	4 ounces	60

DESSERTS

Cakes:

Angel Food Cake	2" piece	110
Cheesecake	2" piece	200
Chocolate Cake (iced)	2" piece	445
Fruit Cake	2" piece	115
Pound Cake	1 ounce piece	140
Sponge Cake	2" piece	120
Shortcake (with fruit)	1 avg. slice	300
Cupcake (iced)	1	185
Cupcake (plain)	1	145

Pudding:

Bread Pudding	$\frac{1}{2}$ cup	150
Flavored Pudding	$\frac{1}{2}$ cup	140

Pies:

Apple	1 piece	331
Blueberry	1 piece	290
Cherry	1 piece	355
Custard	1 piece	280

Counting Calories

Lemon Meringue	1 piece	305
Peach	1 piece	280
Pumpkin	1 piece	265
Rhubarb	1 piece	265
Ice Cream:		
Chocolate Ice Cream	½ cup	200
Vanilla Ice Cream	½ cup	150
Miscellaneous:		
Chocolate Eclair (custard)	1 small	250
Cookies (assorted)	1, 3-inch dia.	120
Cream Puff	1	296
Jello, all flavors	½ cup	78

BREADS & FLOUR FOODS

Baking Powder Biscuits	1 large or 2 small	129
Bran Muffin	1 medium	106
Corn Bread	1 small square	130
Dumpling	1 medium	70
Enriched White Bread	1 slice	60
French Bread	1 small slice	54
French Toast	1 slice	135
Macaroni and Cheese	1 cup	475
Melba Toast	1 slice	25
Noodles (cooked)	1 cup	200
Pancakes, wheat	1, 4-inch	60
Raisin Bread	1 slice	80
Rye Bread	1 slice	71
Saltines	1	17
Soda Crackers	1	23
Waffles	1	216
Whole Wheat Bread	1 slice	55

BREAKFAST CEREALS

Corn Flakes	1 cup	96
Cream of Wheat	1 cup	120
Oatmeal	1 cup	148
Rice Flakes	1 cup	105
Shredded Wheat	1 biscuit	100
Sugar Krisps	¾ cup	110

FISH & FOWL

Bass	4 ounces	105
Brook Trout	4 ounces	130
Crabmeat (canned)	3 ounces	85
Fish Sticks	5 sticks or 4 ounces	200
Haddock (canned)	1 fillet	158
Haddock (broiled)	4 ounces (steak)	207

Counting Calories

FRUITS

Apple (raw)	1 small	70
Banana	1 medium	85
Blueberries (frozen/unsweetened)	1/2 cup	45
Cantaloupe Melon	1/2 melon large	60
Cherries, fresh/whole	1/2 cup	40
Cranberries (sauce)	1 cup	54
Grapes	1 cup	65
Dates	3 or 4	95
Grapefruit (unsweetened)	1/2	55
Orange	1 medium	70
Peach (fresh)	1	35
Plums	2	50
Tangerine (fresh)	1	40
Watermelon	1" slice	60

MEATS

Bacon (crisp)	2 slices	95
Frankfurter	1	155
Hamburger (avg. fat/broiled)	3 ounces	245
Hamburger (lean/broiled)	3 ounces	185
Ham (broiled/lean)	3 ounces	200
Ham (baked)	1 slice	100
Lamb Leg Roast	3 ounces	235
Lamb Chop (rib)	3 ounces	300
Liver (fried)	3 1/2 ounces	210
Meat Loaf	1 slice	100
Pork Chop (medium)	3 ounces	340
Pork Sausage	3 ounces	405
Roasts (beef)		
Loin Roast	3 1/2 ounces	340
Pot Roast (round)	3 1/2 ounces	200
Rib Roast	3 1/2 ounces	260
Rump Roast	3 1/2 ounces	340
Spareribs	1 piece, 3 ribs	123
Swiss Steak	3 1/2 ounces	300
Veal Chop (medium)	3 ounces	185
Veal Roast	3 ounces	230

SALADS & DRESSINGS

Chef Salad/mayonnaise	1 Tbsp.	125
Chef Salad/French, Roquefort	1 Tbsp.	105
Cole Slaw (no dressing)	1/2 cup	102
Fruit Gelatin	1 square	139
Potato Salad (no dressing)	1/2 cup	184
French Dressing	1 Tbsp.	60
Mayonnaise	1 Tbsp.	110